Waiting for Godot

Samuel Beckett

Rosencrantz & Guildenstern Are Dead

Tom Stoppard

Curriculum Unit

Jayne R. Smith

 The Center for Learning

Jayne R. Smith, who earned her B.A. and B.F.A. at the University of Oklahoma and M.A. at the University of Texas, has been acclaimed as an English teacher at Jefferson High School, Port Arthur, and also in southwest and national English conferences. She is the author of a number of Center for Learning units, including *Death of a Salesman, The Martian Chronicles, Walden/A Different Drummer,* and *The Joy Luck Club.*

The Publishing Team

Rose Schaffer, M.A., President/Chief Executive Officer
Bernadette Vetter, M.A., Vice President
Diane Podnar, M.S., Production Director
Amy Richards, M.A., Editor

Cover Design

Robin Smith, B.A.

List of credits found on Acknowledgments
Page beginning on 91.

ISBN 1-56077-243-3

Contents

Introduction

The Theatre of the Absurd leapt into the world after World War II, stunning and confusing audiences with its irrational, illogical depictions of the absurdity of human life. These plays devalued language and stressed what was happening or what was seen or unseen on stage. Audiences did not leave the theatre with a sense of completion; the characters did *not* live happily ever after or die nobly. Sometimes they did not know what happened to the characters or even what happened in the play. But they laughed and thought and discussed and thought. So the plays accomplished their purpose.

Two of the most popular, written a little over ten years apart, are *Waiting for Godot* by Samuel Beckett (1906–) and *Rosencrantz & Guildenstern Are Dead* by Tom Stoppard (1937–). The earlier play has had many thousands of words written about it by critics who take it very seriously. *Waiting for Godot* is one of those works written between 1947 and 1957 on which Samuel Beckett's literary reputation rests. The Irish-born French novelist, dramatist, and poet was awarded the Nobel Prize in Literature in 1969 and the following year his *Collected Works* were published in sixteen volumes.[1]

Far less has been written about *Rosencrantz & Guildenstern Are Dead*, Tom Stoppard's first stage play written in 1967, although it was immediately popular in the theatre world on both sides of the Atlantic. Even the editor of a book of Stoppard criticism is not convinced of the excellence of the Czech-born English playwright whose original name was Tom Straussler and who became a journalist at 17.[2] Perhaps he and others have not seen the seriousness that mixes with Stoppard's exuberance.

Both plays temper their serious subject matter with humor. Neither author tempers his pessimistic view of the modern world. Both plays have great appeal for intelligent high school students.

[1] *Benét's Reader's Encyclopedia*, Third Edition (New York: Harper and Row, 1987), 81.
[2] Ibid., 936.

Teacher Notes

The two plays can be studied individually or together. If both are being used, begin with *Waiting for Godot*, since Stoppard partially based his play on it. Stoppard's play can be read and easily understood without having read Beckett's. However, it does require a knowledge of *Hamlet*, and the poem "Polonius" in **Handout 10** may be used to advantage with *Rosencrantz & Guildenstern Are Dead*, as well as *Waiting for Godot*.

The suggested responses are brief and not necessarily "the truth." Absurdist plays leave themselves open for varied interpretations, a fact that makes group and class discussions lively and interesting. Student discussions and responses should go far beyond the suggested answers. Since the lessons are intended for advanced students, most of the handouts include group work, allowing students to dig for ideas.

The introductory lesson on absurdity calls for the examination of works by three artists, concentrating on René Magritte. The largest collection of Magrittes in America, perhaps in the world, is in the Menil Collection in Houston, Texas. Although slides are not available, the catalog for the 1992 retrospective is available in hard cover and paperback from the Menil and also from the Metropolitan Museum of Art in New York City and the Art Institute of Chicago.

Page numbers are included for both plays, each of which has a standard paperback edition published by Grove Press in New York City. *Waiting for Godot*'s odd pagination—only left-hand pages are numbered—means that numbers have been created here for the right-hand pages, which will be designated by a *B* following the left-hand number (e.g., 29B).

Handout 45, in Lesson 10, is a comparison of the two plays. In the Supplementary Materials are essay topics on each play and on comparing the two plays. These essay topics can be used for writing assignments and for essay tests. (Topic 31 in each topic list is an adapted AP test question.) Essay tests are the best comprehensive and effective way to test students' understanding of these plays. Reading comprehension tests for each play are included, to be used if plays are read outside of class. Short scenes can be read aloud to give an idea of the sounds that lead to the sense.

The 1991 movie version of *Rosencrantz & Guildenstern Are Dead*, written and directed by Stoppard and readily available on videotape, can be used effectively in the classroom because of the changes the author himself made twenty years after writing the play. In the movie, he emphasizes visual images over spoken ones. Students can see the effect of the change of emphasis and evaluate the purpose and the effectiveness.

Magritte Slide Sources

For *Le Blanc-Seing* (*The Blank Signature*) and *La Condition Humaine* ("*The Human Condition*"—a painting on an easel overlooking the ocean it depicts) send note and $3 each to

Office of Visual Services
National Gallery of Art
6th St. and Constitution Ave.
Washington, D.C. 20565

To order the retrospective catalog, *René Magritte* by Sarah Whitfield or the 1992 David Sylvester book (also in bookstores), write to

The Menil Collection
1511 Branard
Houston, TX 77006

Lesson 1
That's Absurd!

Objectives
- To introduce the Theatre of the Absurd
- To show absurd elements in art and literature

Notes to the Teacher

The two major figures in this lesson are René Magritte, the modern artist, and Lewis Carroll, the 19th-century writer and mathematician.

Handouts 1–4 use art. Although black-and-white reproductions are included, the lessons will be far more effective if color reproductions of these paintings (or of similar ones) can be found for students to view. For **Handout 2** a surrealistic painting is included. Ask students to try to locate a color version and prints of Picasso, *Guernica*; *Three Musicians*; M.C. Escher, *Sky and Water II* (in which birds become fish) and other works. Except for *Three Musicians*, these works are in black and white.

A brief list of sources for Magritte is contained in the bibliography in the Appendix. Although he is represented in books about modern art, surrealism, and Belgian artists, many libraries do not have books devoted solely to him. However, his retrospective exhibit in 1992–1993 resulted in several articles in national magazines, all of which included at least three or four color reproductions.

Newsweek (July 6, 1992), describing Magritte as "one of the most pirated artists ever," (the CBS eyeball logo was taken directly from his *The False Mirror*) concluded that "his deadpan succinctness makes him the best surrealist of them all." *Time* (September 21, 1992) noted that the common man in Magritte's paintings, "with his raincoat and bowler, whether standing with an apple in front of his face or floating down in multitudes upon the unperturbed streets of Brussels, really is Magritte—the poker-faced enchanter" and that "no artist ever behaved less like one." A lengthy, pithy Magritte article in the September 1992 issue of *Smithsonian* was accompanied by nine photos of his art.

Some additional Magritte paintings that can be used, ones that are too detailed to reproduce clearly, are *The Key to the Fields* (or others showing a landscape *on* a window instead of through it), *The Human Condition* or *The Fair Captive* (or others showing an easel on which the painting becomes part of its background), *Castle in the Pyrenees*, or *Clairvoyance*, a self-portrait unlike any other. (Don't worry about the titles; they are intentionally non-informative.) Students who often find Magritte's art curiously appealing, will enjoy discussing the absurd and often thought-provoking elements of the titles.

Magritte, the other artists, and Lewis Carroll lead the students to the idea of absurdity, which is "defined" in **Handout 7**. In discussing Carroll, mention that he loved games—just as Vladimir, Estragon, Rosencrantz, and Guildenstern do. His favorite was the monkey puzzle: a monkey on a rope is counterbalanced by a weight. He asks if the weight goes up or down when the monkey climbs. Carroll, like Stoppard, tests the limits of the laws of logic, reducing reasoning to absurdity, using nonsense.

Neither Beckett nor Stoppard claims to be an existentialist (or even to understand fully the philosophy.) Although both plays contain some existential philosophy, neither fits the definition of an existential play. If students are interested in existentialism introduce it at this point. An abbreviated list of beliefs is included in the Supplementary Materials.

Procedure

1. Distribute **Handouts 1** and **2**. Use color prints or photos, if possible. Let students answer the questions as a class. Discuss the simplified definition of surrealism. Answers will depend on the pictures used and the students' ideas and feelings.

2. Distribute **Handouts 3** and **4**. Use color prints or photos if possible. Magritte's comment about "the other side" is much like the Player's comment in *Rosencrantz & Guildenstern Are Dead* about their showing what happens off-stage. Discuss the paintings and Magritte's ideas, which parallel absurdism.

As students discuss the aphorisms, call attention to how #3, 4, and 5 can be applied to the plays. One or more of these aphorisms may be used later as essay questions on one of the plays. As an option, students may choose an aphorism and write briefly on it or use one as a journal entry.

3. Discuss **Handout 5**. Ask a student to read the stanza aloud dramatically. Read paragraph 2. Do students agree? Read the rest of the handout. Discuss Gardner's state- ment as a class.

   The writing of the nonsense poem may be done individually or in groups. Note the warning. People tend to believe anyone can paint a surrealistic painting or write clever nonsense. But both require far more discipline and imagination than writing about or painting the real world.

4. Distribute **Handout 6**. Ask students to read the dialogue from *Through the Looking Glass* silently followed by two students reading aloud the *Waiting for Godot* dialogue. Ask where the comedy lies (word sounds, repetitions, shortness of lines, etc.).

   Read the Carter quote. Ask students to bring it up to date. Recall the 1992 campaign. Can they remember any absurd elements in it? (*One party claimed to stand for family values and had a thrice-divorced actor introduce a major speaker.*)

   If some students have not read either Alice book, offer one or both for free reading or extra credit. Gardner's *The Annotated Alice* adds intriguing notes for the serious reader.

5. Distribute **Handout 7** to students to read silently. Discuss the Theatre of the Absurd, answering any student questions. (Esslin's book is an excellent resource for the teacher.)

6. Distribute **Handout 8**. If possible, show a color print of a Chagall painting. Read and discuss the poem as a light-hearted wrap-up of absurdism.

It's a Bird! It's a Clock! It's Surrealism!

Directions: Sometimes our eyes can deceive us or confuse us. We look at something—a painting, a familiar place—and we recognize certain objects or people or trees, but they are out of kilter. Things are the wrong size or in the wrong shape or don't exist together. This confusion happens in dreams and nightmares. It also happens in art and literature.

Examine the picture in **Handout 2**. What familiar elements do you recognize? How has the familiar been distorted? What effect does the picture have on you?

The art technique is surrealism, which often has dreams as its subject and shows a kind of fantasy in detailed style. Its practitioners consider it not only an artistic process but also a poetic and literary one. It does not allow for reason or morality to interfere in the creation of the art.

Name________________
Date________________

Surrealism

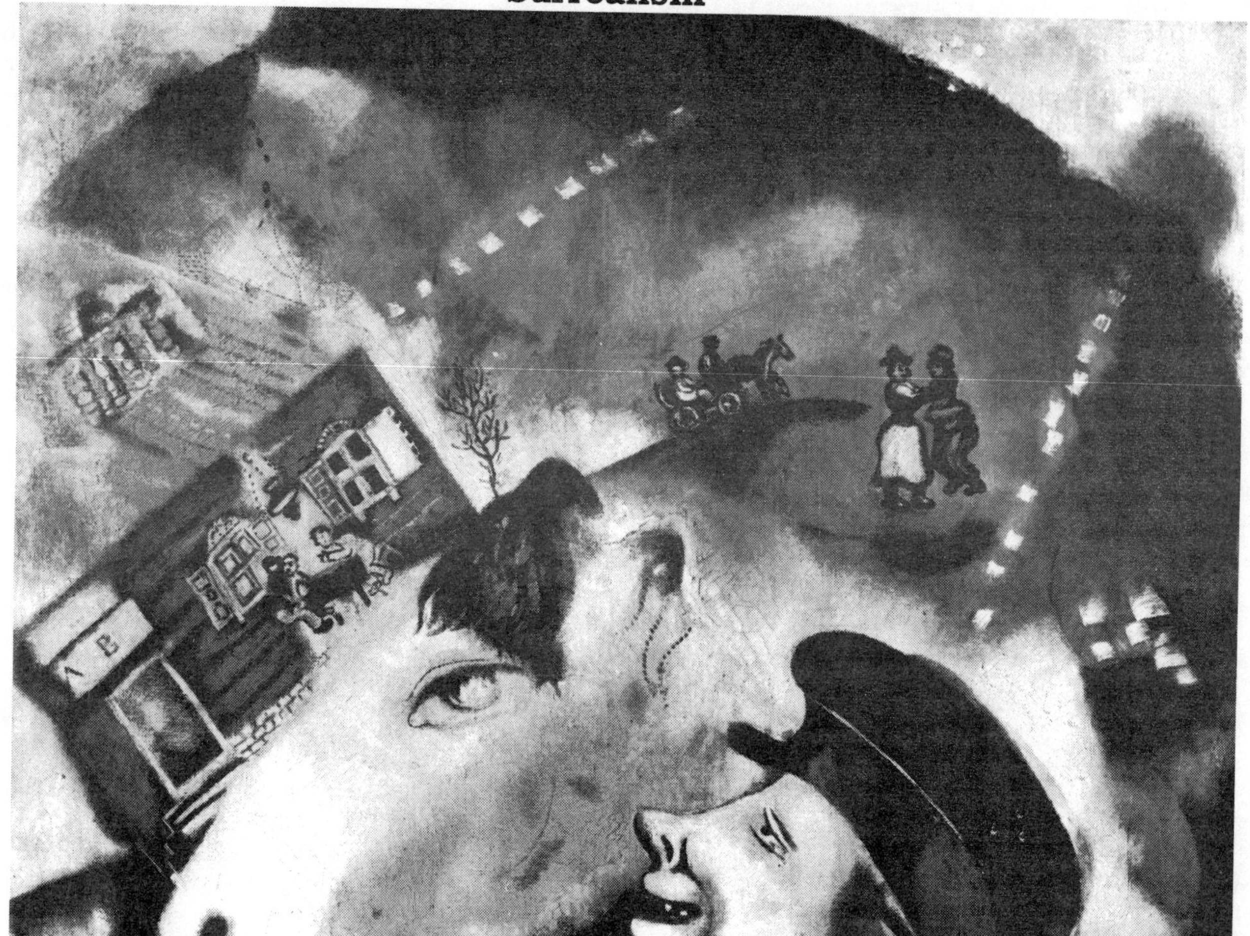

Fig. 1.1 Marc Chagall, *Peasant Life*, 1925, 39 3/8" x 31 1/2", Albright-Knox Art Gallery, Buffalo, New York, Room of Contemporary Art Fund, 1941.

Magritte: The Mystery Man

Directions: Read the following. Examine the paintings in **Handout 4** before discussing the aphorisms.

René Magritte, whose paintings never fail to shock, surprise, or amuse their viewers, often paints visual jokes—a pipe with the words "This is not a pipe" written under it, a crystal goblet containing a giraffe or a man with a hat but no head; some very serious, such as one entitled *The Survivors*, a shotgun, standing in a corner of a room, with blood running out of its muzzle. In 1970 Tom Stoppard, author of *Rosencrantz & Guildenstern Are Dead*, wrote a play entitled *After Magritte* which incorporates some of the jokes in the paintings and some of Magritte's philosophy. Samuel Beckett in *Waiting for Godot*, like Magritte, favors men wearing bowler hats.

Examine Magritte's paintings in **Handout 4**. They contain mysteries, intentional mysteries. They do *not* explain the mysteries or answer the questions brought up by them. The answers are up to the viewer or are perhaps non-attainable. How could anyone explain *Golconde*?

Magritte once wrote, "To equate my painting with symbolism, conscious or unconscious, is to ignore its true nature. People are quite willing to use objects without looking for any symbolic intention in them, but when they look at paintings, they can't find any use for them. So they hunt around for a meaning to get themselves out of the quandary, and because they don't understand what they are supposed to think when they confront the painting. . . . They want something to lean on, so they can be comfortable. They want something secure to hang on to, so they can save themselves from the void. People who look for symbolic meanings fail to grasp the inherent poetry and mystery of the image. . . . By asking 'What does this mean?' they express a wish that everything be understandable. But if one does not reject the mystery, one has quite a different response. One asks other things."[1] Absurdist authors say roughly the same things about their plays. They and Magritte intend to shock and stun us out of our complacency. Magritte once quoted Victor Hugo as saying, "We never see but one side of things." He then said, "It's precisely this 'other side' that I'm trying to express."[2]

As you read each play, especially Stoppard's, see how his ideas are reflected. See how the plays can be considered "surrealistic" (although they do not fit into the category of surrealistic fiction).

Below are some of Magritte's aphorisms. Read each one and decide what you think he means.

1. It is possible to see a tip of the hat without seeing politeness.

[1]Bennett Schiff, "The Artist Who Was Master of the Double Take," *Smithsonian Magazine* (September 1992): 49.
[2]Ibid., 56.

2. An image can sometimes seriously accuse its onlooker.

3. The comprehension of exactitude does not hinder the pleasure of inexactitude.

4. However far one may be from an object, one is never completely separate from it.

5. Whatever the features, words and colours scattered on a page may be, the arrangement obtained always has a meaning.[3]

---

[3]"Lessons by Observation" in *Rhetorique No. 7* Oct. 1962. Qtd. in *Magritte 1992*. New York: te Neus Publishing Co., 1992.

Name_____
Date_____

Magritte's Art

Fig. 1.2. René Magritte, *Golconde*, 1953, 31 1/2" x 39 1/2".

Fig. 1.3. René Magritte, *L'Empire des lumières*, 1954, 51 1/8" x 37 1/4".
Figs. 1.2.–1.3. The Menil Collection, Houston, Texas.

Sounds without Sense

Directions: Read aloud the following nonsense stanza and the interpretative information before writing your own nonsense poem.

> 'Twas brillig and the slithy toves
> > Did gyre and gimble in the wabe:
> All mimsy were the borogoves,
> And the mome raths outgrabe.[4]

This is the first stanza of Lewis Carroll's famous nonsense poem from *Through the Looking Glass*, "Jabberwocky." Read it aloud with feeling. It sounds logical enough—the sentences are correctly structured for the English language. You can tell what part of speech each word is (can't you?), and you can tell that a scene is being set with some actions taking place. Yet none of the key words make any sense!

Humpty Dumpty later explains to Alice the meanings of the hard words: " 'Brillig' means four o'clock in the afternoon—the time when you begin *broiling* things for dinner. . . . 'slithy' means 'lithe and slimy'. . . . 'toves' are something like badgers—they're something like lizards—and they're something like corkscrews. . . . a 'rath' is a sort of green pig."[5]

Needless to say, these definitions and his others, as well as the poem itself, leave us in the same confusion we were in when looking at surrealistic paintings. Yet, they may also give us the same pleasure.

Martin Gardner, an eminent mathematician and games maven as well as the annotator of *The Annotated Alice*, notes, "There is an obvious similarity between nonsense verse of this type and an abstract painting. The realistic artist is forced to copy nature, imposing on the copy as much as he can in the way of pleasing forms and colors; but the abstract artist is free to romp with the paint as much as he pleases. In similar fashion the nonsense poet does not have to search for ingenious ways of combining pattern and sense; he simply adopts a policy that is the opposite of the advice given by the Duchess in [*Alice in Wonderland*]*—he takes care of the sounds and allows the sense to take care of itself. The words he uses may suggest vague meanings, like an eye here and a foot there in a Picasso abstraction, or they may have no meaning at all—just a play of pleasant sounds like the play of non-objective colors on a canvas."[6]

*The Queen, quite unsoundly, says, "Take care of the sense, and the sounds will take care of themselves," parodying the British proverb, "Take care of the pence and the pounds will take care of themselves."

Just for fun: Try writing a nonsense poem of your own. You can use the structure of "Jabberwocky" or of some other familiar poem or you can create your own form. Be true to English sentence structure and use real structure words such as *the, and, that, is,* etc. Make it sound logical. A warning: nonsense is hard to write, just as surrealistic paintings are hard to paint; you have only your imagination to rely on.

[4]Lewis Carroll, *The Annotated Alice* (New York: Clarkson N. Potter, Inc., 1960), 270.
[5]Ibid., 270–272.
[6]Ibid., 192.

Name_____
Date_____

That's Absurdity

Directions: Read the following quotes. Be prepared to discuss a current event that could be classified under the term "absurd."

Absurd dialogue from *Through the Looking Glass*:

> Here the Red Queen began again. "Can you answer useful questions?" she said. "How is bread made?"
>
> "I know *that*, Alice cried eagerly. "You take some flour—"
>
> "Where do you pick the flower?" the White Queen asked. "In a garden or in the hedges?"
>
> "Well, it isn't *picked* at all," Alice explained; "it's *ground*—"
>
> "How many acres of ground?" said the White Queen. "You musn't leave out so many things."[7]

Absurd dialogue from *Waiting for Godot*:

ESTRAGON: What do we do now?

VLADIMIR: While waiting.

ESTRAGON: While waiting.

VLADIMIR: We could do our exercises.

ESTRAGON: Our movements.

VLADIMIR: Our elevations.

ESTRAGON: Our relaxations.

VLADIMIR: Our elongations.

ESTRAGON: Our relaxations.

VLADIMIR: To warm us up.

ESTRAGON: To calm us down.

VLADIMIR: Off we go.

Both are almost slapstick comedy. The Absurdists want us to see life as a kind of absurd comedy, a surrealistic painting with familiar elements in unfamiliar places.

Notice what Martin Gardner, writing about metaphor in the Alice books, says: "Life, viewed rationally and without illusion, appears to be a

[7]Ibid., 322.

nonsense tale told by an idiot mathematician. At the heart of things science finds only a mad, never-ending quadrille of Mock Turtle waves and Gryphon particles. For a moment the waves and particles dance in grotesque, inconceivably complex patterns capable of reflecting on their own absurdity. We all live slapstick lives, under an inexplicable sentence of death. . . . "[8] The last sentence could serve as an introduction to both plays.

Absurd politics

During the 1992 Presidential campaign columnist Hodding Carter III wrote, "What has been going on is utterly unexplicable, an absurdist play in which the lead characters talk past each other, and the set, constructed for drama, clashes with the nonsense downstage."[9]

Can you think of any current or recent election or news event that can be described in similar terms?

[8]Ibid., 15.
[9]NEA Syndicate, New York, September 6, 1992.

Name_____

Date_____

Theatre of the Absurd

Directions: Read the following characteristics of the Theatre of the Absurd.

When Alice goes into the woods where things have no name, she asks, "Who am I?" This question of identity is common in absurdist theatre.

Theatre of the Absurd shows a "sense of the senselessness of the human condition and the inadequacy of the rational approach by the open abandonment of rational devices and discursive thought."[10] The emphasis is on the situation instead of the event. It doesn't pretend to give a moral or even have a thesis. It usually even lacks a plot. It merely presents the absurdity of the human condition. Reality often merges into fantasy; language and reason often dissolve; characters lack any apparent motivation; things happen that are not rational. The actions do not happen in logical ways. The plays are often humorous.

Theatre of the Absurd relies upon the image. Since it is purely subjective, it also relies upon the reader or viewer to incorporate his or her own feelings and experiences into the play. As a result no one, no matter how expert, can state what a play means.

Because stage images are so important, you must read the stage directions carefully and try to visualize the setting and the movements. Also notice the author's directions for timing, such as "Silence" or "Beat." Silences can be as important as speeches in the Theatre of the Absurd.

[10]Martin Esslin, *The Theatre of the Absurd* (New York: Doubleday and Co., 1961), xix–xx.

A Poet Gets Absurd

Directions: Read the following poem and answer the questions.

Absurdity is not limited to painters and playwrights. Poets practice it too. (Who can forget Gertrude Stein's "A rose is a rose is a rose?")

Lawrence Ferlinghetti, a Beatnik poet of the 1950s, was inspired by paintings by Marc Chagall, a Russian whose dreamlike paintings of his childhood village contain horses, violins, upside-down peasants, and many other sane and absurd images, to write this poem.

Don't Let That Horse

Don't let that horse

eat that violin

cried Chagall's mother

But he

kept right on

painting

And became famous

And kept on painting

The Horse With Violin In Mouth

And when he finally finished it

he jumped up upon the horse

and rode it away

waving the violin

And then with a low bow gave it

to the first naked nude he ran across

And there were no strings attached[11]

1. What makes the poem absurd?

2. Where is the humor in the poem?

[11]Carol Marshall, *Twentieth Century Poetry* (Boston: Houghton Mifflin, 1971), 48–49.

Lesson 2
Literary Absurdity

Objective
• To introduce key ideas in the play through poetry

Notes to the Teacher

Just as art and nonsense-writing show absurdity, so does poetry. This lesson introduces the ideas of emptiness, identity, and the unknown future which are common to the Theatre of the Absurd and to the two plays.

Copies of the Eliot poems are not included since they appear in many English literature anthologies or poetry collections. If students have already studied the poems, they can answer the questions and relate them to the play. If they have not read either poem, use only one of them for this lesson.

Miroslav Holub, author of "Polonius," has written many powerful, unusual poems, many of them about the aftermath of war. He, like Magritte, is largely unrecognized and unantho- logized. (This poem is an excellent one to use as a writing assignment for AP students as they study *Hamlet*.)

If you wish, give different handouts to three different groups (four if you use both Eliot poems) for students to work on during class time. Conduct a session in which groups share their responses.

Procedure
1. Distribute **Handouts 9** and **10**. If students have not read "The Hollow Men," read it aloud as they follow in their books. If they have already read it, allow time for them to skim the poem before they jot down answers for the questions. Discuss the answers. Use same procedure for **Handout 10**.
   Suggested Responses, **Handout 9**:
   The Hollow Men
   1. *Their dependence on others, inability and unwillingness to act, fear of the eyes of reality, barren land (and lives), inability to pray, etc.*
   2. *"Groping together," "headpiece filled with straw," "behaving as the wind," "dead man's land," etc.*

Prufrock
1. *Inability to ask the question, his indecision, worry about appearance, fear of death, "Do I dare to eat a peach?", etc.*
2. *"I have measured out my life in coffee spoons," "The butt-ends of my days and ways," "a pair of ragged claws," etc.*

Suggested Responses, **Handout 10**:
1. *Answers may include Holub's emphasis on Polonius' spying tendencies and general worthlessness.*
2. *Slinks, oozes, floats, stab*
3. *Stanza 3 suggests sugar-coated activity; "boneless," "wax flesh," "mousy," and "jellied flunkey" in stanza 4 characterize Polonius not as sweet, but plastic, irrelevant, nothing.*
4. *Nothing; "a bird will chirp in gratitude." The world will be a happier place, a heavy weight having been lifted.*

2. Distribute **Handout 11**. Read the poem aloud. Let students work in groups.
   Suggested Responses:
   1. *The armless ambidextrian, lighting a match as an act, the lion biting a woman's neck, coughing in waltz time, swinging Jocko by the thumb*
   2. *It sets you up for something and then reminds you of it after a long insert. It also uses understatement to lead to the extraordinary event of the top blowing off.*
   3. *Life*
   4. *"Starless dark," "vast wings," "canceled skies"*
   5. *It can be devastating—there is nothing after life. Or the sense of vastness can be an overwhelming and awesome idea.*

Emptiness

Directions: T.S. Eliot, in his well-known poem "The Hollow Men," describes the emptiness of modern man. He believes we live in an era without values and without emotions.

This idea of emptiness is echoed not only in many Absurdist plays but also in many other poems, such as Eliot's "The Love Song of J. Alfred Prufock."

Read either (or both) of these poems and answer these questions:

1. How does Eliot show the emptiness of the person(s)? (actions, statements, etc.)

2. What images does he use to suggest emptiness?

3. How valid is his statement for today's world?

Name_____
Date_____

Identity

Directions: "Who am I" is a common problem in many Absurdist plays. But sometimes the real problem is that the person is not who he thinks he is. Read this poem by Miroslav Holub, a Czech poet and scientist, about a familiar character from *Hamlet*.

Polonius

Behind every arras
he does his duty
unswervingly.
Walls are his ears,
keyholes his eyes.

He slinks up the stairs,
oozes from the ceiling,
floats through the door
ready to give evidence,
prove what is proven,
stab with a needle
or pin on an order.

His poems always rhyme,
his brush is dipped in honey,
his music flutes
from marzipan and cane.

You buy him
by weight, boneless,
a pound of wax flesh,
a pound of mousy philosophy,
a pound of jellied
flunkey.

And when he's sold out
and the left-overs wrapped
in a tasseled obituary,
a paranoid funeral notice,

And when the spore-creating mould
of memory
covers him over,
when he falls
arse-first to the stars,
the whole continent will be lighter,
earth's axis straighten up
and in night's thunderous arena
a bird will chirp in gratitude.[1]

[1]*Selected Poems* (Baltimore: Penguin Books, 1967) 73–74.

1. Polonius considered himself wise and prudent. The king trusted him implicitly. How does Holub show him?

2. What verbs emphasize his character?

3. What contrast is shown in stanzas 3 and 4?

4. What will remain of him after his funeral? How does this relate to the theme?

Name_____
Date_____

What Is in the Future?

Directions: Read this poem. With your group, jot down answers to the questions.

The characters in both *Waiting for Godot* and *Rosencrantz & Guildenstern Are Dead* are constantly wondering what is ahead. Of course no one has read the script of his life; no one knows what, if anything, lies ahead.

Archibald MacLeish reveals a pessimistic view of the future in his poem about an absurd circus.

The End of the World

Quite unexpectedly as Vasserot
The armless ambidextrian was lighting
A match between his great and second toe
And Ralph the lion was engaged in biting
The neck of Madame Sossman while the drum
Pointed, and Teeny was about to cough
In waltz-time swinging Jocko by the thumb—
Quite unexpectedly the top blew off.

And there, there overhead, there, there, hung over
Those thousands of white faces, those dazed eyes,
There in the starless dark, the poise, the hover,
There with vast wings across the canceled skies,
There in the sudden blackness, the black pall
Of nothing, nothing, nothing—nothing at all.[2]

1. What elements of the circus are absurd?

2. What is the effect of repeating "quite unexpectedly" in the first and eighth lines?

3. What is the circus a metaphor for?

4. What phrases describe the "nothing" that remains? Why are they effective?

5. What is the emotional effect of having the end of the world lead to "nothing at all"?

[2]Laurence Perrine and James M. Reid, eds., *100 American Poems of the 20th Century* (New York: Harcourt, Brace, Jovanovich, 1966), 162–163.

Lesson 3
Two Tramps at Twilight

Objectives

*   To lead students into reading *Waiting for Godot*
*   To establish the difference in the two characters

Notes to the Teacher

Martin Esslin, in *Theatre of the Absurd*, tells of a 1957 presentation of *Waiting for Godot* to 1,400 San Quentin prisoners. The apprehensive director told the convicts to think of the play as they did jazz, to listen for what each one found in it, his own personal significance. The convicts not only understood the play, but also were deeply moved by it. They understood waiting and the futility of waiting. They were not bothered by the lack of plot, development, and logic.[1] (An essay topic deals with this.)

Tell students to read the play in the same spirit and not to worry about what it does *not* have. **Handout 12** is intended to lead them into the play by having them make assumptions and ask questions.

Since the play lacks all the conventions of standard theatre, answers to interpretative questions will—and should—vary greatly. There are no right answers.

In **Handout 12**, question 1, students are likely to ask: *Who is speaking? Where are they? Done about what? Why is Vladimir changing his mind? Why can nothing be done?*

In **Handout 15** make sure that their comparisons are complementary ones that balance.

Procedure

1. Distribute **Handout 12**, to be done during class, *before* handing out copies of the play. Ask several to read aloud their dialogues. Collect the handouts and keep them until students have read the play. Assign the reading of the play.

2. After students have read the play aloud or as homework, return **Handout 12**. Were their questions answered? Were their assumptions correct? Distribute **Handout 13** for students to answer the questions in class discussion.
    Suggested Responses:
    1. *We have no clues about where Vladimir goes. Estragon was in a ditch the night before act 1. He won't say where he was the next night.*
    2. *Because they're waiting for Godot*
    3. *They have hope that he will come.*
    4. *Probably not—unless Godot comes*
    5. *It would probably be circular, as are the play and Vladimir's song.*

3. Distribute **Handout 14**. Talk about the excess of names and the fact that the Russian's other name is English while the Frenchman's other name is Latin. The three names per person may suggest their confusion or the fact that their identity is vague or that they are both Everyman and no man. There are further identity problems in telling carrots from turnips, in remembering the color of Estragon's boots, and in the characters failing to recognize or remember the others when they reappear.
    Suggested Responses:
    1. *He wanted to suggest that the characters are all of us everywhere; the play shows the condition of the world. Pozzo's answering to both Cain and Abel (53) also contributes to this; Estragon says, "He's all humanity (54). In act 1, when asked who they were, Estragon says, "Adam" (25). In act 2, when asked who they were, Vladimir says, "We are men" (52).*
    2. *Vladimir is bossy, like a ruler. Estragon, like an herb, is more earthy (he likes to sit on the mound). Pozzo's translated name suggests his less-than-admirable character. Lucky can be either an ironic name or an appropriate one: perhaps he is lucky to have a known position in life, with someone in charge and somewhere to go.*

4. Distribute **Handout 15** to be done in small groups or as homework. The traits are complementary ones (good/bad, tall/short, etc.).

---

[1]Martin Esslin, *Theatre of the Absurd* (New York: Doubleday Publishing Co., 1961), xv.

21

Suggested Responses:

Vladimir	Estragon
1. breath	feet
2. hat	shoes (fit in act 2)
3. is upset by them	likes to tell them
4. likes them better (i.e., carrots)	likes them less
5. won't listen to them	wants to describe them
6. remembers them	forgets them immediately
7. has faith	is skeptical
8. stronger; sometimes protective	volatile, dull, slow to enthuse
9. high-strung, persistent	weaker; often beaten up
10. optimistic, serious, practical	pessimistic, forgetful, lazy, says he was a poet, has less
11. an intellectual	need of knowledge
12. prostate trouble (urination)	bad feet

13. Because of their complementary traits they must depend on each other and stay together.
14. a. They are old.
    b. There is no light (knowledge) coming to them.
    c. Time is passing quickly.
    d. Night lies ahead, not day (which could be Godot).
15. They are unchanged, unaffected by any of the happenings. They exist only in the present.
16. No, they are inextricably tied together.

22

Getting Started

Directions: Read the following and answer the questions.

ESTRAGON: Nothing to be done.

VLADIMIR: I'm beginning to come round to that opinion.

These are the opening lines of *Waiting for Godot.* Without reading any further in the play, do the following exercises.

1. Write five questions that you can ask based on the two lines.

2. What clues are there about the character of each speaker?

3. How do you expect a play that starts this way to end?

4. Write a continuation of this dialogue, one that you think could logically follow (no more than one page).

Shall We Go?

Directions: Read the following and be prepared for class discussion of the questions.

In the previous handout you anticipated the ending of the play. Were you on the right track?

Now reread the last two lines and stage direction.

> VLADIMIR: Well? Shall we go?
>
> ESTRAGON: Yes, let's go.
>
> (*They do not move.*) (60B)

These were, of course, the last two lines of act 1 as well as of act 2. Both acts begin with a grand reunion (so apparently they *do* go somewhere each night; we know Estragon is beaten each night.)

1. Are there any clues as to where they go?

2. If they do go somewhere and separate, why do they so obviously not go at the end of each act?

3. What does their not going seem to suggest?

4. Will they ever be able to go beyond the tree (and their unseen sleeping places)? Why or why not?

5. If they ever were to move, how meaningful will their movement be? What shape would it be?

Notice that the stage directions on the first two pages of act 2 say five times that Vladimir "comes and goes." Notice also that Estragon alone opens act 1 as Vladimir alone opens act 2.

What's in a Name?

Directions: Read the following helpful information. Jot down answers to questions for use in class discussion.

Their nicknames make them sound like a pair of dancehall girls, Didi and Gogo. But they also have two other names. Vladimir answers to "Mr. Albert" when the boy speaks and Estragon confesses to be named Catullus. Which are first names and which are surnames no one knows. What might be the purpose of this excess of names?

The names have translatable meanings:

Vladimir, a Russian name, means "ruler of the world."

Estragon, in French, is the herb tarragon.

Pozzo, an Italian name, means "pool"; in common use it means "cesspool." (It is pronounced *pot*-zo.)

Lucky has an English or American name with an obvious meaning. (Pozzo refers to him as a "knook," which apparently is a king's jester or fool—a wise fool.)

1. Why do you suppose Beckett—an Irishman who moved to France, wrote all his plays in French, and then translated them into English—chose names from four different countries? (We are ignoring ancient Rome.) By what other identities or names do they answer to or refer to themselves as?

2. In what ways are the names appropriate or significant?

Together Wherever We Go

Directions: Although the two tramps are good friends who cannot separate from one another, Beckett has created them as two distinctly different people. As you will see, as you fill in the chart below and answer the questions, they have complementary characteristics.

	Vladimir	**Estragon**
1. What stinks		
2. What hurts		
3. Reaction to funny stories		
4. Reaction to things he gets used to		
5. Reaction to dreams		
6. Remembrance of past events		
7. Faith in Godot to change things		
8. Temperament		
9. Degree of strength		
10. Key traits		
11. Intelligence		
12. Physical problem		

13. What is the importance of their traits being complementary?

14. What is the significance to the fact that we only see the two at twilight?

15. How do the two change during the play?

16. They frequently talk about leaving each other. Will they ever be able to do this?

Lesson 4
The Absurd Universe

Objectives
- To discover the absurdity in the play
- To reveal the themes of identity and alienation
- To note the humor in the play

Notes to the Teacher

This lesson delves into a few of the absurd elements in the play, leaving room for further delving. The absurdist playwright presents man's absurd human position without comment and without logical order or reasoning, but this element is not the focus of this lesson nor are the lack of apparent motivation and character development. These ideas may be discussed prior to doing the handouts.

Lucky's wild speech is not paraphrasable and has no definite meaning although it suggests many things. Three Latin words in the beginning do have meanings: *apathia*: apathy; *athambia*: a lack of capacity for terror or amazement; *aphasia*: speechlessness, which attacks Lucky after his speech. The "stuttered" words *Acacacacademy* and *Anthropopopometry* suggest not only intellectual knowledge but also *caca* and *popo*, children's words for excrement, also suggested by the Cackon country, where they are (40).

Procedure

1. Distribute **Handout 16**. Allow students to read the introductory material. Divide the class into groups to discuss the questions. If preferred, give **Handouts 16–18** to different groups for discussion and brief presentations to the class of their responses.
   Suggested Responses:
   1. *Each act opens with one character on, one off (different ones each act). The endings are identical except for speakers. In both acts Pozzo and Lucky arrive; the boy brings a message from Godot; Estragon tells of being beaten, Vladimir worries with his hat; Vladimir and Estragon discuss suicide; they wait for Godot.*
   2. a. *VLADIMIR: I'm afraid he's dying.*
         ESTRAGON: It'd be amusing (53B).
      b. *ESTRAGON: Yes, let's go.*
         (They do not move.) (60B)
      c. *POZZO: Where have I put my pipe?*

   LUCKY: Charming weather we're having (23).
   3. *They deteriorate and degenerate. The suitcase now has sand in it instead of possessions. Pozzo is blind, Lucky dumb. This degeneration takes time.*
   4. *Everyone—landlord, slave, tramps—is dressed alike, illogically. The absurd switches with Lucky's hat in act 2. Vladimir's constant peering into and shaking of his hat; the smashing of Lucky's hat.*
   5. *The pieces of chicken, half-eaten, that Estragon picks up off the floor and eats make him look absurd as well as starved. They also point out the serious absurdity of the rich man tossing bones to the poor man. The vegetables are rarely the ones being searched for and are not what one expects in someone's coat pocket.*
   6. *It is their relationship—the boss and the human packhorse, both apparently content; Pozzo's extreme ill-treatment of Lucky.*
   7. *They make no progress.*

2. Distribute **Handout 17**. Ask students to read silently the section preceding the questions. Briefly discuss the question, whose answer, to Beckett, was apparently "Yes!" Divide the class into groups to discuss the numbered questions. Share group responses. Questions 2 and 3 may be used for writing assignments. The purpose and effect of silences and pauses in the play may be an interesting topic for a writing assignment.
   Suggested Responses:
   1. *Several things: The scholar with no substance; the intellectual or artist controlled by the non-intellectual or non-artist in the absurd world; people who rely totally on others; masochists; exploited people who accept their exploitation; those who cannot bear the burden of freedom (followers of Jim Jones, who committed suicide when he told them to)*
   2. *He loses his pipe, to great distress, his throat spray, his watch, and his sight. Probably most of the rest of his possessions went with his sight. He keeps Lucky,*

now dumb. He makes up an excuse for his watch—he must have left it at the manor, though he had used it just a few minutes earlier. The losses show there is no permanence in possessions and the futility of tyranny.

3. Distribute **Handout 18**, which groups together identity and alienation. Ask students to read the introduction. Discuss the meanings of *identity* and *alienation*. Divide the class into groups for discussion.
   Suggested Responses:
   1. *It suggests a loss of identity; sameness or lack of uniqueness of people. If they are everyone, they are also no one.*
   2. *The four are, in a sense, interchangeable. (See pp 22B, 27B, 28, 30, and 46 for main uses.) Each thinks there is a uniqueness about the hats, but they are the same.*
   3. *Pozzo kicking Lucky; Estragon kicking Lucky; Vladimir and Estragon ignoring Pozzo's pleas for help; Estragon falling asleep during conversations*
   4. *There are several types of falls: the pratfalls of all characters in act 2 (49B, 52, 52B, 54B, 55) and the slapstick falling of Estragon's pants (60); Estragon's near-falls (13B, 38, 43); his falling into Vladimir's arms (47, 47B); Pozzo's falls (54B, 55); night falling (51B, 58). Falling suggests a going away, a distancing. The characters keep falling or almost falling, suggesting their inability to survive unsupported; night falling suggests invisibility, fear, separation, and perhaps death.*
   5. *Friends mistreat each other. Vladimir cannot do things that the slave Lucky can do. Pozzo and Lucky's situation is merely a game for them. The reunion scenes show how alienated the two are from the rest of the world. The only familiar object to them is the other person.*

4. Distribute **Handout 19**. Read aloud the samples of humor. Assign each row of students a group of pages to search for humorous lines or actions to read to the class. Make sure that students realize that the laughter mingles with the sadness of man's condition.
   Suggested Responses:
   Some of the circus games include the routine

with the boot (which is also mime), the falling pants, Vladimir's dashes offstage, the exercises, the mass fall in act 2, the reaction to the other's smell, Vladimir's flea in his hat, Vladimir, Estragon, and Pozzo all taking off their hats simultaneously in order to think and then putting them on together.

The clown acts are ways they use to avoid their unceasing boredom. Note that on p. 48B, as they abuse each other by calling names, Estragon wins with "Crritic!"—an author's comic revenge.

Name_____
Date_____

The Absurd World

Directions: Read the introductory paragraph. With your group members, discuss the questions.

> Vladimir and Estragon live in an absurd world, a meaningless world, populated by a barren tree and a low mound (usually a large stone in productions). The tree miraculously—absurdly—grows four or five leaves overnight. Pozzo and Lucky appear out of nowhere and leave to go "on." A messenger appears briefly. No one else inhabits their world. They have no home, no possessions except their clothing.

1. It is a world of circular motion. Their lives are a repeated cycle of meaningless activity and talk. In many ways, acts 1 and 2 are just alike, suggesting the cycle. What are some of the ways in which they are alike?

2. The actions (or non-actions) of the play are just as important as the words. One of these is the frequent silences. Sometimes the actions or non-actions do not fit with the words. For example, in the opening scene Estragon says, "Nothing to be done" but he continues his long struggle with his shoes. What other examples of disjunctive words and/or actions can you find?

3. What happens to Pozzo and Lucky overnight? Why is this absurd?

4. How are the bowler hats used for absurdity?

5. What is absurd about the food in the play (the raw vegetables and the chicken bones)?

6. What is absurd about Pozzo and Lucky?

7. How far do Vladimir and Estragon progress in the course of the play?

Ships That Pass in the Night

Directions: Read the section preceding the questions. With your group members, discuss the numbered questions.

> Pozzo: You are human beings none the less. . . . Of the same species as myself"
> (15B).

> Pozzo: I am perhaps not particularly human, but who cares? (196).

> Human or not, Pozzo responds to calls of both "Cain" and "Abel" with "Help!", causing Estragon to say, "He's all humanity" (53B–54). What a frightening thought! Are humans sadistic, tyrannical, thoughtless, possessed by their possessions, awed by their own power, desperate for attention? Beckett does not paint a complementary picture.

1. Lucky, the submissive slave, carries the luggage (and the whip), wears a rope around his neck, obeys his master's every trivial order. He dances (no longer very well) and thinks (no longer very clearly) for his master. Pozzo intends, in act 1, to sell him at the fair, as a kindness. Who or what can Lucky represent?

2. Pozzo is the typical landowner and slaveholder, a man immensely proud of his possessions. Trace specifically what happens to his possessions in the course of the play, including Lucky. How does he comfort himself for any of his losses? What do the losses show?

3. After Lucky, who used to do many dances, does his dance of the net, he speaks for the first and last time. His speech is as entangled as a net, its shouted words, a mixture of sense and nonsense, in one Joycean sentence. It sounds like a college lecture delivered in jabberwocky. Can you determine what he says about heaven? man? the earth?

4. Does Pozzo change in act 2? Explain.

Name_____
Date_____

Haven't I Seen You Somewhere Before?

Directions: Read the introduction. With your group members, discuss the questions.

Instead of identical bowler hats à la Magritte and Charlie Chaplin, all four characters often need glasses or hearing aids. "Pozzo" sounds like "Godot" to Estragon. One day after seeing each other, no one recognizes anyone else. Pozzo, of course, has an excuse, although he doesn't remember meeting anyone. Estragon doesn't remember the place. When the boy returns in act 2, looking exactly the same, he claims he wasn't there the previous day and has seen none of them before. Near the end of act 1, after Pozzo and Lucky leave, Vladimir suggests that they have seen them before although Estragon doesn't know them. Estragon says, "Why didn't they recognize us then?" Vladimir replies, "That means nothing. I too pretended not to recognize them and then nobody ever recognizes us" (32). As he talks to the boy, Vladimir seeks reassurance: "You did see us, didn't you?" (34).

1. What does this lack of memory, of recognition, suggest about modern life?

2. What does the sameness of the hats, Vladimir and Estragon's vaudevillian hat exchange, and routines with Lucky's hat suggest about identity?

3. In act 1, Vladimir and Estragon turn from sympathizing with Lucky to attacking him verbally. This can be called an act of alienation. Their distance from both men makes any emotional reaction insincere, based on lack of knowledge and a basic lack of interest. Find other instances in which characters seem alienated from one another.

4. The motif of "falling" ties in with alienation. Find a number of examples of people or things falling or almost falling. Decide the purpose of this motif and how it connects with alienation. Include "nightfall" and "falling into someone's arms."

5. Vladimir and Estragon play a game in which they pretend to be Pozzo and Lucky, Estragon calling Vladimir "pig" just as Vladimir called him the same a few pages earlier. Vladimir is told to think and to dance. He can't do either. How does this scene show alienation? Twice during the scene Estragon goes off stage, is missed, returns, falls into Vladimir's arms, the second time occurring about one minute after the first. Vladimir says, "There you are again at last" and, the second time, "There you are again again!" How do these reunion scenes show alienation?

Humor of Absurdity

Directions: Read the samples of humor. In the pages assigned to you, search for humorous lines/actions.

Although the comedy is very obvious when this play is presented, some people fail to catch much of the humor in this tragicomedy when they read it. Some is subtle, some broad, some slapstick. Some of their short, snappy dialogue is styled after English music halls, in which cross-talk is performed, similar to the routines of Abbott and Costello: one man speaks intelligently; the other man doesn't get it or misunderstands. The lines are fast and funny but delivered with poker faces. Often one performer breaks into song, as Vladimir does. Beckett also incorporates mime techniques (Estragon's long mime of taking off his boot, for example) and circus clownery—pratfalls, funny clothes, falling pants, etc. Vladimir and Estragon name the three types of humor on page 23B.

Some examples of humor:

1. VLADIMIR: Go to hell.

   ESTRAGON: Are you staying there?

   VLADIMIR: For the time being (52B).

   Note that Estragon's line has a double meaning because of the ambiguous word *there.*

2. (Vladimir and Estragon are trying to escape from the stage in desperation. Vladimir pushes Estragon towards the audience. Estragon recoils in terror. Vladimir looks at the audience.)

   VLADIMIR: Well, I can understand that (47B).

3. Pozzo looks at his watch to see how many years have passed.

4. VLADIMIR: We are not saints, but we have kept our appointment. How many people can boast as much?

   ESTRAGON: Billions.

See what other lines and actions you can find that make the play humorous.

Lesson 5
A Meaningless World

Objectives
- To introduce the theme of meaninglessness
- To become aware of the emptiness of the characters' lives
- To emphasize related themes and symbols

Notes to the Teacher

In this lesson, all of the handouts deal directly or indirectly with the theme of meaninglessness, a theme students should grasp intuitively and find both interesting and depressing to discuss. The final handout is a writing exercise giving students an opportunity to apply Beckett's philosophy to their own world.

None of the answers is absolute, allowing many questions to lead to arguments with defenses deriving from the text.

Procedure
1. Distribute **Handout 20**. Divide students into groups for discussion. Questions 1 and 2 can be linked using students' selected lines from the poem to parallel the lines from the play. Two examples are given.
   Suggested Responses:
   1. *Both groups go nowhere in circles, are repetitive, fail to act, have slim hope, and are untouched by reality. Vladimir and Estragon end each act with a whimper and no bang.*
   2. a. *(It is repeated four times.) He gives up, makes no effort.*
      b. *Inaction preferable to action ("Not that final meeting . . . ")*
      c. *Inability to act; lack of motivation*
      d. *Lack of emotions ("Lips that would kiss form prayers . . . ")*
      e. *Indecision, urge for individuality but inability to accept it*
      f. *Inaction, lethargy*
      g. *Escape from individuality, decision-making*
      h. *Lack of purpose or interest*
   3. *Their empty talk fills in the empty time, keeps them from thinking and from hearing the voices of the dead (the past? 40-40B).*

4. *They are probably more hollow. Vladimir and Estragon have something to look forward to, faith that Godot will come. Pozzo and Lucky are wrapped up in themselves.*
5. *They show the unlikelihood of Godot's ever coming and an unpleasant view of the man their hopes rest in.*
6. *The desire for suicide suggests that death is preferable to their life. The hollow men envy those who go "with direct eyes" to death, who don't wait on the shore, unable to cross. Notice the rope that drives Lucky goes around his neck, suggesting suicide.*
7. *Hope*

2. Distribute **Handout 21**. Discuss the introduction. The broken cord, in terms of what happens in the play, probably does not mean that they are not tied together, but it could. It may also show the fragility of their relationship. They probably are tied to Godot who is their only hope. Discuss questions 1 and 2 as a class before dividing to complete the handout. Share the group responses.
   Suggested Responses:
   1. *The two pairs of men are tied to the forces that keep them moving—even if their movement is in circles. They are perhaps tied to their place in the universe by unseen forces that control them. They are tied in because they have no choice.*
   2. *Yes. A life tied to a person, a place, or situation with no reason and no chance of escape is a meaningless one. Dylan Thomas, in "Fern Hill," says that though he was chained to the force of time as a child, "I sang in my chains like the sea."[1] In the play, the men chafe, chatter, play games, get confused, remove shoes, and wait.*
   3. *It is the monotonous cycle of life that gets neither worse nor better.*
   4. *They will discuss hanging but will not perform it.*
   5. *(See pp. 22B, 24B, 30B, 55B.) Time originally is an obsession. He has to get somewhere on time; his watch is a tie*

[1] *Collected Poems of Dylan Thomas* (New York: New Directions, 1957), 178.

with the past when perhaps time meant something; his lost watch reduces his importance and meaning. When blind, he says, "The blind have no notion of time. The things of time are hidden from them too" (55B). He is less firmly oriented than Vladimir.

6. Nothing can stop time's passing. They may accomplish nothing while passing the time, but time still passes; there is no escape from time.

7. The speech is somewhat similar to Macbeth's "tomorrow and tomorrow" speech, also about the futility of life. One's life is a brief gleam, a candle, and then it is gone, unremembered, unimportant, just like the men's lives. Not only will no one else remember them, but they will not remember each other.

(*Note:* Students might enjoy comparing the play's philosophy to Macbeth's in this speech.)

8. Earlier Vladimir says, "One can bide his time. . . . No further need to worry." Estragon replies, "Simply wait." Vladimir: "We're used to it" (25B). They have nothing but time. Through his gravedigger and forceps speech, he shows that birth and death balance each other.

3. Distribute **Handout 22**. Reach agreement that the *tree* is a symbol. If preferred, the other words may be called *motifs*. Beckett himself saw Vladimir as belonging to the tree, as light oriented towards the sky while Estragon "is on the ground, he belongs to the stone."[2]

Suggested Responses:

1. Perhaps hope, since it blooms in act 2, or the leaves can merely mean the cycle of time continues or that nature survives and flourishes while man is doomed to die.

2. The earth, lower ideals and functions (i.e., Estragon's stories)

3. Perhaps they represent hope for improvement, since the shoes fit in act 2. At the end of each act Estragon leaves the shoes at the front of the stage, almost like an offering; they may make someone with smaller feet happy.

4. The passage of time, the possible approach of an end

5. Man's possessions with which he is burdened

6. Man's urge for power and domination

7. The sameness in people

8. The games are part of the meaninglessness of their routines and their lives. Most are pointless time-wasters, especially imitating the tree.

9. Perhaps in their lives they are playing roles with no scripts (as Rosencrantz and Guildenstern do). Pozzo is most impressive when he is most insincere—even his emotions are meaningless.

4. Distribute **Handout 23**. Allow time for students' questions. Assign for homework with several days to complete the edited draft. During the writing process, arrange for peer reading and editing of the opinion paper. If possible, allow them to edit in class.

[2]Linda Ben-Zvi, *Samuel Beckett* (Boston: Twayne Publishing, 1986), 142.

They Are the Hollow Men

Directions: As a member of your group, discuss the following questions. Be prepared to share your group's views with the class.

> They are waiting.
>
> As they wait, they carry on pointless conversations and play silly games. They have nowhere to go and nothing to do. They are the hollow men Eliot wrote about, living in an empty world.

1. Draw parallels between the characters in the play and the poem. (Omit discussion of religious parallels since they will be discussed in the next lesson.)

2. How do these lines suggest their hollowness:

   a. VLADIMIR: Nothing to be done (8).

   b. ESTRAGON: Don't let's do anything. It's safer (12B).

   c. POZZO: I don't seem to be able . . . (*long hesitation*) . . . to depart (31).

   d. VLADIMIR: You don't know if you're unhappy or not?

      BOY: No, sir.

      VLADIMIR: You're as bad as myself (34).

   e. ESTRAGON: I sometimes wonder if we wouldn't have been better off alone, each one for himself. . . . We weren't made for the same road (35).

   f. VLADIMIR: We can still part, if you think it would be better.

      ESTRAGON: It's not worth while now (35B).

   g. VLADIMIR: We're in no danger of ever thinking any more.

      ESTRAGON: Then what are we complaining about? (41B).

   h. ESTRAGON: I'm tired breathing (49).

3. Vladimir and Estragon talk constantly. How is this fact connected with hollowness or emotions?

4. Are Pozzo and Lucky less hollow than Vladimir and Estragon? Why or why not?

5. How do the messenger's statements add to the emptiness?

6. How do their attempts at suicide add to it?

7. What is the one thing that Vladimir and Estragon have going for them?

Time and "Tied" Wait for No One

Directions: Read the introduction in preparation for discussion before joining your group to complete the handout.

Lucky, like a trained animal, is driven by his circus master, Pozzo, by means of a rope; later, as the dumb leading the blind, he guides him by a shorter rope. Either way, they are tied together for life.

Estragon removes the cord that successfully holds his pants up in order to commit suicide. The cord breaks when they pull on it. Does this mean they are not tied together?

In act 1 Estragon asks Vladimir if they are tied to Godot. Vladimir is confused by the question and then says, "What an idea! No question of it. (Pause) For the moment" (14B). Does this mean they *are* tied to him? Notice that just after they discuss this, Lucky enters, tied to an invisible (at first) master.

1. What is the significance of the use of *tied*?

2. Does being tied contribute to emptiness and meaninglessness? If so, how?

Time is another theme that wanders through the play. *Wanders* is an apt word since time does not really pass, although the moon comes out after the sun sets, and we see a second day. When you wait, time moves very slowly. And they are waiting. And waiting. *Waiting* is the key word in the play. Apparently not only the waiting but also time will stop when Godot arrives. They will be "home," safe from the endless cycle of time that they have been experiencing, time with no scheme, no shape, time that is eternal and repetitive.

3. Both pairs of men have been together for a long time, fifty and sixty years. The implication is that nothing has changed in any of their lives or in their relationships in that period. How does this fact connect with the idea of emptiness and meaninglessness?

4. Vladimir and Estragon say they'll hang themselves tomorrow unless Godot comes. What implications can you make about their future life if Godot does not come?

5. Pozzo, when he first appears, shows off his watch and checks it often. Then he loses his watch. Examine the scenes with the watch and decide what they reveal. What does he say about time in act 2, when he is blind? How firmly oriented in time is he?

6. In act 1, when Pozzo consults his watch, Vladimir says, "Time has stopped." Pozzo assures him it hasn't (24B). When Pozzo and Lucky leave, Vladimir says, "That passed the time." Estragon replies, "It would have passed in any case" (31B). What do these lines suggest?

7. When the blind Pozzo asks what time it is, Vladimir and Estragon examine the sky, give two possibilities, look at the sunset, and Estragon says the sun is rising. Vladimir finally assures Pozzo it is evening. Vladimir is concerned about whether Pozzo and Lucky are the same men who came yesterday. Pozzo finally says, "Have you done tormenting me with your accursed time!" and continues with his "one day" speech (57B), ending with "They give birth astride of a grave, the light gleams an instant, then it's night once more." Explain this speech and its significance.

8. On p. 58 Vladimir wonders about tomorrow. "What shall I say of today?" Then he repeats part of Pozzo's speech, including a gravedigger with forceps. What does he mean when he says, "We have time to grow old"?

Name_____

Date_____

Words, Words, Words

Directions: *Symbol* may be too limited a term for some of the repeated words in the play, but we will use it anyway. By observing their use in the play, what do each of these symbols represent?

1. tree

2. mound (or stone)

3. shoes

4. moon

5. luggage

6. whip

7. hats

8. Vladimir and Estragon play games often during the play: word games, circus games, abusing each other (48), the tree (49), exercises. What do these games suggest?

9. Vladimir and Estragon pretend to be Pozzo and Lucky, making them actors. Pozzo delivers a speech about the sky—complete with lyrical voice and dramatic pauses; then he turns to Vladimir and Estragon for dramatic criticism. Even Lucky has his strange moment on stage. What does Beckett suggest through this acting motif?

Name_____
Date_____

How Goes the World?

Directions: Beckett presents the reader with an absurd world devoid of meaning. The characters lead repetitive, meaningless lives. Pozzo gives a definition of life: "They give birth astride of a grave, the light gleams an instant, then it's night once more" (57B).

This was Beckett's view of the world in 1953, four decades ago. Does our world still fit his description? Is life meaningless? Are we all merely waiting for something or someone who will probably be a disappointment when and if he or she comes?

Think about these questions. Decide on your position. Write a paper defending your position, using specific examples from today's world as proofs. If you cannot decide on a definite position, if you see two or more sides, choose one anyway and defend it as if you did support it.

If the world is too large a subject, you can limit your paper to America, your state, your town, your school—any portion of the world you have experienced or know about.

You need not mention the play, but you may use quotations from it if you wish. Do not discuss the play. This is an opinion paper.

Lesson 6
Religion

Objectives
- To clarify the religious references in the play
- To discover Beckett's attitude toward religion

Notes to the Teacher

The author, Beckett, forces the reader to consider the religious aspects through his characters' discussion of the two thieves and other comments involving religion. Avoid using discussion as a forum for students' beliefs; make them concentrate on Beckett's, with assurance that they do not have to believe as Beckett does, but they do need to understand what he implies.

Some critics find the play an affirmation of faith: the tree sprouts leaves, the shoes suddenly fit. But everything else suggests an arbitrariness about God, a cruelty, a lack of caring—much like Dr. T.J. Eckleberg, the billboard "god" in the waste land of *The Great Gatsby*.

In **Handout 25**, question 6 may be used as a basis for writing. The idea of *grace* may need some explanation to help some students understand aspects of Beckett's views.

Procedure

1. Distribute **Handout 24** for students to read before class discussion. "Ah" suggests "awe."

2. Distribute **Handout 25**. Discuss the introduction before students group for discussion.
   Suggested Responses:
   1. *God arbitrarily favored Abel as Godot arbitrarily favors the boy, and one thief was rather arbitrarily saved.*
   2. *He planned to sell Lucky instead of kicking him out, perhaps in order to gain favor or grace with God. Instead he does not sell him, and he goes blind. There is no implication that the blindness was a punishment, but it can be.*
   3. *Martin Esslin summarizes it nicely: "God, who does not communicate with us, cannot feel for us, and condemns us for reasons unknown."[1]*

4. *The first is a comic exaggeration. The second suggests that Estragon sees his situation as a slow death; he is being crucified daily but not quickly.*
5. *The new shoes*
6. *Essentially, he is shown as often cruel, arbitrary, and uncaring.*

3. Distribute **Handout 26**. Refer students again to "The Hollow Men." Point out any additional parallels.
   Suggested Responses:
   1. *Not quite. It suggests that religion may be their hope, but that they cannot even complete a prayer; religion may not be a valid "cure."*
   2. a. *Only the hope of empty men—merely a hope, not a possibility*
      b. *The hope of empty men only—not something others would hope for*
      c. *The only hope of empty men—their only hope for salvation*

      Godot can be seen in all three ways; like the hollow men, the characters do not know which version is valid.
   3. *They have forgotten their religion or they are insincere. They haven't enough energy or concern to complete a complaint, much less a prayer. In the play, "We're waiting for Godot" and "Ah" becomes almost a prayer. Complaints are common. Neither accomplishes anything.*
   4. *Pozzo puts his faith in his power and his possessions. Vladimir trusts in his vague appointment with Godot. Lucky worships his master. Pozzo and Lucky's faiths are misplaced. Perhaps Vladimir's is, too.*

---

[1]*The Theatre of the Absurd* (New York: Doubleday and Co., 1961), 22.

Name_____

Date_____

Who Is Godot?

Directions: Read carefully the following before writing your interpretation.

Godot = God. This equation seems obvious to most people. Not to Beckett. He said, "If I knew, I would have said so in the play."[2] You have been warned.

Who or what can he be?

- a supernatural being?

- a mythical superman?

- a savior?

- whatever we may long for in life?

Every time Vladimir says, "We're waiting for Godot," Estragon replies, "Ah." (There is one exception.) What does the "ah" sound like?

Vladimir and Estragon did not ask Godot for anything very definite, and Godot did not promise anything. That is not a very firm basis for hope. If they are hoping to have a person with authority to lead them, then they would be in Lucky's position, which would make their hope and waiting meaningless. "Their situation, then, is that of people waiting for nothing much, in a universe that has nothing much to offer."[3] The waiting may be mere habit, something that keeps them from facing reality.

Godot, although blessed with a beard that may be white, is not kind and loving. He beats the messenger's brother who keeps the docile sheep and is pleasant to the boy, who keeps the wayward goats. He feeds his keepers fairly well. He expects people to be patient and willing to wait interminably. If he is God, he is not the God we like to picture. He is quite arbitrary. The coming of Godot is not necessarily good: Estragon thinks, "I'm accursed" and runs away when he thinks he is coming perhaps to punish him.

What is your interpretation of Godot?

[2]Martin Esslin, *The Theatre of the Absurd* (New York: Doubleday and Co., 1961), 12.
[3]Eugene Webb, *The Plays of Samuel Beckett* (Seattle: University of Washington Press, 1974), 29.

Name_____
Date_____

One Was Saved

Directions: After class discussion of the following introduction, join your group for discussion of the questions.

Religious references occur frequently in the play. These do not necessarily make it a religious play or a play about religion. Most likely it includes comments on religion.

Very early in the play Vladimir and Estragon discuss the story of the two thieves on the cross with Jesus. One was saved and the other damned—very much like the messenger and his brother. Vladimir is disturbed because only one evangelist wrote about the saving of one. But he says, "One of the thieves was saved. . . . It's a reasonable percentage" (8B). What amazes Vladimir and Beckett is the chance element—one thief out of millions happened to be at that spot on that day and to make the remark that saved him. It was sheer chance—the chance that made Pozzo, not Lucky, the ruler.

Vladimir suggests that they repent. Estragon says, "Our being born?" This seems to be what they are suffering for.

1. Pozzo answers to both "Cain" and "Abel" in act 3. How does the play incorporate a parallel to the Cain and Abel story?

2. Grace is the bestowal of God's blessing on some; it, not man's acts, decides who is to be saved. People hope for salvation through grace. What act of Pozzo's may be intended as an attempt to achieve salvation? Was it successful?

3. How does Lucky describe God in his speech?

4. Twice the word *crucify* is used when Vladimir attacks Lucky for mistreating poor Pozzo: "Crucify him like that!" Later Estragon says he has compared himself to Christ all his life. Vladimir, missing the point, says, "But where he lived it was warm, it was dry!" Estragon replies, "Yes. And they crucified quick." What does the use of *crucify* show?

5. What happening concerning Estragon may be considered an act of grace?

6. If Godot is God, what does the play suggest about God?

Religion and Hollow Men

Directions: Refer again to Eliot's "The Hollow Men." Find the references to religion. What do they say about religion and the hollow men? The following questions will help you formulate your answer.

1. Does the play make the same point about religion that the poem makes?

2. Look at this line in the poem, referring to the symbols of religion: "The hope only of empty men." By moving only one word, the same word each time, write this phrase three ways so it has three different meanings. What are the meanings? Connect these meanings to the play.

3. Near the end of the poem, the hollow men's attempts to pray are interspersed with their complaints about life's length. Why are the attempts at prayer incomplete? How do both prayers and complaints connect with the play?

4. The hollow men pray to broken stone. In what sense does Pozzo pray to broken stone? Vladimir? Lucky?

5. Some say that any meaning in life has to be made by oneself. Do you agree? Why or why not?

Lesson 7
Hamlet Inside Out

Objective
- To become aware of Stoppard's use of *Hamlet* in *Rosencrantz & Gildenstern Are Dead*

Notes to the Teacher
Rosencrantz & Guildenstern Are Dead loses most of its effect and much of its humor if the reader/viewer is not familiar with *Hamlet*. Therefore, this play is best taught immediately after a study of *Hamlet*, although it can be taught later with references to Shakespeare's *Hamlet*.

Bits and pieces from Shakespeare's drama appear throughout Stoppard's play. *Rosencrantz & Guildenstern Are Dead* will help the student recognize these borrowings and find purpose in their use. It includes a "turn-around" writing assignment for the student to reveal creativity, understanding of both Rosencrantz and Guildenstern and the work being parodied, and perhaps the ability to use wit and wordplay.

Advanced students should be capable of reading the play on their own. As it is discussed in class, let students read short scenes aloud in order to hear the sparkle of Stoppard's language. Call attention to the question game in act 1 and the second speech of p. 67, ending with the wonderful line, "Stark raving sane." Note that the lines move much more quickly and are much funnier than in *Waiting for Godot*.

Procedure
1. Distribute **Handout 27** before the students read the play. It provides information about sources of the play and tells them what to look for as they read.

2. After they have read the play and taken a comprehension test, distribute **Handout 28**. If convenient, divide the class into three groups, one to a question, with each group choosing a spokesman to report its discoveries. The questions are designed to initiate the topics rather than merely to answer the questions.
   Suggested Responses:
   a. The *Hamlet* scenes given in some detail are those in which Rosencrantz and Guildenstern appear in the original play but in which nothing significant is said.

   b. The most important scenes, such as "To be or not to be," are reduced to total insignificance or absurdity. Hamlet speaks only thirty times in the entire play. Most of his characterization is established through stage directions, especially in act 3.

   c. Stoppard uses the pantomime of Shakespeare's dumb show to act out several key scenes.

   d. Scenes off-stage in Hamlet (Ophelia's closet, the boat) are on-stage in Rosencrantz & Guildenstern Are Dead.

   e. Rosencrantz and Guildenstern, who rarely appear in Hamlet, never leave the stage.

   f. Serious scenes seem humorous when they appear upstage or out of context.

   g. Stoppard gives Hamlet no personality, no depth. In act 3, the furthest removed from Hamlet, he becomes a vaudeville comic, spitting into the audience, jumping into barrels.

   h. Stoppard has Rosencrantz and Guildenstern disappear on stage instead of dying off-stage, although he includes the final scene from Hamlet.

   i. The questions game and many other questions in the play are suggested by the frequent questions in Shakespeare's play, many of them are Hamlet's, the "interrogative mood"[1] of Hamlet's world, according to Maynard Mack's essay, "The World of Hamlet." Rosencrantz, in act 3, scene 3, compares the death of a king to a wheel. Hamlet's speech to the players comments on art. The King and Queen's apparent confusion when they first speak to Rosencrantz and Guildenstern suggests their interchageability. Hamlet's hawk and handsaw speech suggests the pair's confusion about direction.

   j. The first view of Hamlet is of a madman, doublet unbraced, etc. The last view is of his leaping into a barrel. This is not the sober, thoughtful, dignified Hamlet.

[1]*Hamlet* (New York: New American Library, 1963), 237.

k. *In act 3, which is, in a way, an acting out of what is merely told about in Hamlet, Hamlet is characterized not by what he says (which is nothing) but by his actions, dress, and manner.*

l. *Stoppard includes or alludes to both the sponge scene and the recorder scene (112). "To be or not to be" is reflected in act 3 with the discussion based on "You can't not-be on a boat."*

3. Distribute **Handout 29** as a creative writing assignment. Allow time for peer editing and rewriting. Read aloud some of the final drafts.

4. If students view the movie version of *Rosencrantz & Guildenstern Are Dead*, they will discover that Stoppard has inserted far more scenes from *Hamlet* than he used in his play. Several are significant scenes. If dumb shows, pantomime, and summaries of plot are counted, only about 13 of the play's 126 pages come from Shakespeare, whereas at least 20 percent of the movie borrows from Shakespeare.

Name_____

Date_____

Hamlet Who?

Directions: Read this guide before you read the play to alert you to the focus of your attention as a means of understanding the author's ideas or questions he poses.

Recipe

Take one famous tragedy. Shake well.

Scoop off the main characters who float to the top. Set aside.

Pick out the two smallest characters remaining.

Blow these up with hot air.

Let them float through your play as the heroes.

Toss main characters in lightly and in small amounts.

Serves all who enjoy laughing while they think.

This recipe describes what Tom Stoppard, author of *Rosencrantz & Guildenstern Are Dead,* did to create his intriguing play. As the Player explains, they "do on stage things that are supposed to happen off," while all of the significant actions in *Hamlet* occur offstage or in brief pantomime upstage (which is the rear of the stage). Notice how this parallels Magritte's idea of showing the other side of things.

The play can also be described as a mathematical formula: *Hamlet + Waiting for Godot = Rosencrantz & Guildenstern Are Dead*. You will find both obvious and subtle bits and scenes from *Hamlet* and both obvious and less obvious borrowing from *Waiting for Godot,* the most significant of which is the pair of characters who are always on stage, always confused and uncertain.

Poor Hamlet is no more than a walk-on in the play. As you read, watch for his appearances and determine from what scene in *Hamlet* each one comes. What very important scenes are reduced to a line or two or to a brief mime?

You may think of the play as the revenge of Ros and Guil, who are frequently omitted entirely from productions of *Hamlet*. You may have noticed their absence in Mel Gibson's movie version which also omitted the Players. Rosencrantz and Guildenstern are also missing from Laurence Olivier's classic movie version.

As you read, also notice Stoppard's use of major themes and motifs. The play is dense with them. Notice these for future discussion.

Themes	**Motifs**
death	games
identity	messenger/calling
alienation	boat
life as a game	home
exits and entrances	wheel
acting vs. reality	direction
	coins

Like George Bernard Shaw, Stoppard's stage directions are very important; read them carefully.

By the way, Stoppard, who was born in Czechoslovakia in 1937, pronounces his name *stow-pard*, with both syllables equally accented.

Hamlet by the Ounce

Directions: Now that you have read this topsy-turvy version of *Hamlet*, you can see the comparisons, the changes, the manipulations, and the humor. You can also see the play is far more than a revised version. Your group will be assigned one of the following topics. Take notes which include page numbers so that you can give specific examples when you share your ideas with the class. A copy of *Hamlet* will be helpful for reference.

1. Stoppard's choice of scenes: Which scenes did he choose? Why? Which ones are given in some detail? Why? Which ones in brief form or mime? Why? How are these scenes used in the play? In what act is *Hamlet* almost non-existent? Why? Which scenes have elements that suggest lines, actions, or ideas in *Hamlet?* For example, what is the source for the questions in *Rosencrantz & Guildenstern Are Dead?* for the wheel imagery? for the Player's comments about art? for Rosencrantz and Guildenstern's confused identity? etc. Where is "to be or not to be" suggested?

2. Stoppard's *Hamlet* humor: Where does the reader/viewer who knows *Hamlet*, laugh at something that would not be funny to someone else? Where does incongruity cause humor? Where does Rosencrantz and Guildenstern's inability to understand something Hamlet or other characters say cause humor? Where does Stoppard humorously mix the two plays? In what ways has Stoppard turned *Hamlet* into Theatre of the Absurd?

3. Stoppard's Hamlet: Examine the Hamlet seen and heard in *Rosencrantz & Guildenstern Are Dead.* How would you characterize him? How is he seen in act 3? Why doesn't he speak? In what ways has Stoppard changed him? Why? Is he in any sense a hero? Is he absurd?

Name_____

Date_____

Up from the Minors

Directions: You too can be a Stoppard. Think of a well-known play or novel you have read or studied. Shake it well, scoop off the main characters, and find a minor character hiding at the bottom.

Some examples: *Macbeth*: a witch or Lennox or Ross; *Death of a Salesman*: Bernard or Willy; *Pride and Prejudice*: Lydia; *The Scarlet Letter*: Pearl; *Lord of the Flies*: Percival or Roger.

Choose a scene from that work. Put your character downstage center figuratively, and retell the scene with him or her as the main character. No matter what the form of the original, you may write either in play or story form.

Be sure to include major characters in a minor way. Be true to the original plot, but your character can go beyond the plot, as Rosencrantz and Guildenstern do. If you can, be witty.

Lesson 8
Who Are Rosencrantz and Guildenstern?

Objective
- To focus attention on the identity problem

Notes to the Teacher

This lesson deals with identity, perhaps the major theme of the play. The psychological questions "Who am I?" has been discussed and argued for untold years. Stoppard has created not an *I* but a *we*. Rosencrantz and Guildenstern, who may be two sides of the same coin or perhaps the same side of two coins, want to know who they are but are doomed never to know. Students are intrigued by the idea of identity and can be encouraged to discuss their own search for identity or books or movies that deal with the problem.

Magritte has several paintings suggesting a loss of identity which can be used as a starting point for discussion. Among them are *Not to be Reproduced, Golconde, The Lovers, The Month of Harvests*, and *The Therapist*. These depict such things as heads covered by cloths, missing heads (sometimes replaced by a bird cage), and masses of identical people.

There are no right-wrong answers to most of the questions. Rosencrantz and Guildenstern are the protagonists and the Player serves as the Greek chorus with Delphic powers (he knows how the play ends).

As students discuss Rosencrantz and Guildenstern's characters, read this apt quotation from Tom Prideaux in *Life* "Rosencrantz & Guildenstern Are Dead proves to be an apt expression of our dilemmas and doubts. . . . Uncertainty is a sign not necessarily of a weak and wavering mind but often of a venturous mind prying out truths not simple to assess."[1]

Incidental information: The Rosencrantz and Guildenstern families were both very important in Denmark for several hundred years. One Rosencrantz was Danish governor of Bergen, Norway, in the mid-1500s and has a still-standing tower named after him and a 20th-century

hotel. Ros would be delighted!

Procedure
1. Distribute **Handout 30**. Discuss briefly the term *protagonist*. Discuss, as a class, the questions in paragraph 1. In small groups, discuss the numbered questions. All are opinion questions whose answers call for supports.

Suggested Responses:
2. *Life or society or no antagonist*
5. *They suffer; they are defeated at the end. They are not noble for they have no tragic flaw, etc. They fulfilled their obligation in life—to perform or to serve—or they passed up their chance to be heroes by not destroying the letter they read. Like anti-heroes, they lack most heroic virtues, especially courage, but they do not lack honesty. Unlike anti-heroes, they are not worried about traditional values; their worries are more immediate.*

2. Distribute **Handout 31** as homework. Discuss answers in class. The two men are very hard to tell apart. (In the movie version they are much easier to keep apart in terms of character.)

Suggested Responses:
1. *and 6. are Guildenstern; 2–5 are Rosencrantz.*
7. *Guildenstern is intellectual, searching for logical answers; Rosencrantz is somewhat dense and slow to catch on. The differences are not particularly significant; Stoppard wants to keep the audience somewhat confused, just as his characters are.*
8. *Dependence on each other, curiosity, fear, ignorance (not knowing), and ability with words*
9. *Act 2, scene 2. The Queen reverses the order of their names.*
10. *See Notes to the Teacher.*
11. *To point up modern man's lack of identity*

[2]Tom Prideaux, " 'Who are we?' 'I don't know.' " *Life* (February 9, 1968): 76.

3. Distribute **Handout 32**. See Notes to the Teacher for possible lead-ins to the exercise. Divide students into small groups for research and discussion.
   Suggested Responses:
   1. *In addition to obvious mix-ups about their names, included should be their inability to recognize themselves in the two actors playing them, the humorous lines about Hamlet's confusing them (104) and their "Which is which?" (121) followed by "Who are we?" (122). If they don't know who they are, they cannot resolve any of their other problems. Their lives are meaningless.*
   2. *The first two humorously muddle religious identities. No one is who he seems to be. The third shows that even obvious identities are not certain.*
   3. *The I changes to we, making the two men one. One man's fate is the other's—and perhaps everyone's. The Player seems to suggest that the fact that they exist is enough.*
   4. *On p. 64, the Player says the actors pledged their identities, "secure in the conventions of our trade, that someone would be watching." They lose their identity when they lose their audiences. Their identity seems to be the role they are playing. Only poor Albert is ever seen outside his role, except for the Player. Yet even the Player is always in costume, always "on." The Player says at one point, "We're the opposite of people."*

4. Distribute **Handout 33** to be done as homework. Point out that Stoppard uses *direction* in two ways:
   a. instructions
   b. which way: north, east, etc.
   Suggested Responses:
   1. *References occur on pages: 20, 39, 58, 72, 80, 85, 86, 100, 102, 112, 120, 122. The boat can change direction; they cannot.*
   2. *When one merely follows directions—or does nothing for lack of directions—he is not being an individual.*
   3. *They don't know where they are or who they are or why they are where they are. They never leave the stage, until they disappear. Without an identity they cannot move.*

5. Distribute **Handout 34**. Ask students to read the first three paragraphs silently. Discuss some of the questions. Divide the class into groups of three to five to write skits which they will perform. Turn in the final draft for evaluation. Warn them against using real people unless they are famous ones far removed from the local community.

Where Is the Protagonist?

Directions: Discuss the questions in paragraph 1. In your group, discuss the opinion questions. Support your answers.

In *Hamlet* we have no doubt as to who the protagonist and tragic hero is. But what about in *Rosencrantz & Guildenstern Are Dead*? Who is the hero? Is there a hero? Can a non-entity be a protagonist? Is there an antagonist working against a protagonist? If so, who is he? If not, can you have a protagonist without an antagonist?

Some people say Ros and Guil are the protagonists since they are at stage center and never leave. Others claim the Player is the protagonist since he is a philosopher and seems to know where he, and everyone else, is going. Others say the play is heroless, that Stoppard is defining the modern world as a place where heroes do not exist.

1. What is your position? Be able to defend it.

2. Who is the antagonist? (It need not be a person.) Defend your answer.

3. Does the protagonist come to self-knowledge in the end? If so, when?

4. Is Stoppard showing a world in which heroes do not—or cannot—live? Why or why not?

5. If you were to consider Rosencrantz and Guildenstern as the protagonists, what do they have in common with tragic heroes? How do they differ? In what sense are they anti-heroes?

6. In act 3, when they read the letter from the King, they have a chance to act, to do something heroic, but they choose to do nothing. One critic says they have chosen to be cowards. Do you agree or disagree? Why?

7. Do you identify with Rosencrantz and Guildenstern at any point? Do you agree with critics who call them Everyman? Why or why not?

Telling the Difference

Directions: Answer the questions and be prepared to discuss them in class.

Ros and Guil have a serious identity problem: they don't know who they are. And no one else can tell them apart either, although they do not look alike. Has Stoppard created identical characters or are they distinguishable?

1. Who seems more intelligent?

2. Who is concerned about hurting someone else?

3. Who is more worried about death?

4. Who gets confused when one pretends to be Hamlet?

5. Who is "only good in support"?

6. Who has a dominant personality, according to the other?

7. What conclusions can you draw about each character from the answers? Characterize each briefly. Are their differences significant in terms of the play?

8. What character traits do they have in common? Are these traits significant?

9. What scene in *Hamlet* suggested to Stoppard that the two were difficult to tell apart?

10. A coin is used frequently in the play. In what way can it symbolize Rosencrantz and Guildenstern?

11. What is Stoppard's purpose in having characters who are almost identical?

Identity Problems

Directions: Read the following introduction about the theme of *identity*. With your group, research and discuss the questions.

In the existential world, identity is a major problem. In today's world people are constantly searching for an identity. "Who am I?" remains a key question.

Stoppard has chosen identity as a major theme in his play. Two men who don't know which name to answer to certainly have a problem.

Hamlet opens with a problem of identity. Neither guard recognizes the other, perhaps because it is dark:

BERNARDO: Who's There?

FRANCISCO: Nay, answer me. Stand and unfold yourself. (1.1)

Rosencrantz and Guildenstern would be baffled. Who should they say is there? Would they give the right names? Could they "unfold" (disclose) themselves?

1. Throughout the play, from their first attempt to introduce themselves to the players, to their disappearance at the end, Rosencrantz and Guildenstern are unsure about their identity ("Is that you?" "Yes." "How do you know?" [97]). Find as many examples as you can of their confusion. Determine Stoppard's purpose in having their identities confused.

2. How do Ros's stories about Saul/Paul, a Christian, a Muslim, a Jew, and the Chinese philosopher tie into the identity problem?

3. On p. 122, after Guil reads the letter condemning them to death, Guil asks, "But why? Was it all for this? Who are we that so much should converge on our little deaths? Who are we?" the Player answers. "You are Rosencrantz and Guildenstern. That's enough." Explain what this interchange means. Is there any significance in the switch from "Who am I?" to "Who are *we*?" If so, what is it?

4. Think about the Player and his troop in terms of identity. Do the Tragedians have identities? If so, what are they? Who is the Player? When are they "on"?

5. The existentialists, among others, believe modern man has lost his identity. Do you believe this play proves their thesis? Prove your answer.

Where Am I?

Directions: As individual homework, think through and answer the following problem questions.

Hamlet gave Rosencrantz and Guildenstern a strong hint about his pretended madness, but they did not pick it up: "I am but mad north-northwest: when the wind is southerly I know a hawk from a handsaw" (2.2). However, Stoppard picked up his direction motif, which is part of the identity question, from this line.

1. Find the many references to (1) directions, or (2) direction, starting with Guil's early complaint: "We are entitled to some direction" (20) and including their attempts to determine what direction they came from or are going towards.

2. Several references to directions occur. The men are following directions throughout. They were "sent for." A messenger appeared, called their names, and they came. They don't know why they were called. But they know they had no choice at any time. How does this tie into identity?

3. They long to go home but have lost their sense of direction . They aren't even sure where the sun is. They often intend to leave ("Should we go?" "Where?" "Anywhere") but they go nowhere. How does this loss of direction tie into identity?

4. Must a person have an identity before he can make choices? Why or why not?

Who Am I?

Directions: Read and discuss the examples below before writing your group skit.

> In a recent *Calvin and Hobbes* cartoon, Calvin admires shirts and logos or product names on them. He tells Hobbes, "It says to the world, 'My identity is so wrapped up in what I buy that *I* paid the *company* to advertise its products!'" and explains, "Endorsing products is the American way to express individuality" (August 27, 1992).

> Three teenaged girls shop at the mall for something to show their individuality. All buy the same T-shirt.

Our identities are our individuality. You can undoubtedly think of many ways in which you, your friends, or your national leaders have lost their identities without realizing it or are totally confused as to who they are. Do they show their uniqueness by dressing like everybody else? by listening to the same CD's? or by styling their hair in the latest mode? Do they think for themselves? Do they have ideas? Do they parrot others' ideas? Do they dare to eat a peach?

In groups, write comic skits (one per group) that illustrate common identity problems. Have at least three characters in your skit. Once you have created a first draft, work on the dialogue to make the lines witty. Use wordplay such as Stoppard uses (puns, twisted clichés, word switches, etc.).

Practice the skits and perform them for the class.

Lesson 9
Themes

Objectives
- To become aware of the worlds represented in the play and their significance
- To delve into the meanings of the themes of death, acting, and alienation

Notes to the Teacher

As a Theatre of the Absurd play, *Rosencrantz & Guildenstern Are Dead* contains no morals, no solutions, no arguments. It merely presents the absurdity of Rosencrantz and Guildenstern's predicament. Thus, the themes that permeate it are difficult or impossible to pin down and explain logically. The absurd world cannot be reasonably explained.

As a result, in this lesson both the questions and answers given allow a lot of leeway for individual interpretation. The questions asked will lead to other questions, with questions being as important as answers. (Both *Hamlet* and *Rosencrantz & Guildenstern Are Dead* suggest this.) Students answers should go far beyond those posed, with disagreements likely.

The ultimate goal is to motivate students to think, discuss, and even argue. They will undoubtedly note that Stoppard's key themes, death and acting, are also major themes in *Hamlet*, as are such elements as questions, reality, and alienation.

If the entire play analysis is done by group discussion and panels instead of individual lessons, **Handouts 36** and **37** deal with death, **37–38** with acting, and **39** with alienation. The game in **Handout 40** can be played at any point. **Handout 35**, a writing assignment, can be distributed as students work on their panels, or it can be done as homework.

Handouts 36–39 may be used as group or class discussions or distributed to four different groups for discussion with informal group presentations followed by class discussion.

Procedure
1. Distribute **Handout 35**. Ask students to read it carefully and to discuss the ideas in it.

Assure them that there are no right-wrong answers about the worlds.

Allow time for a free-write on "Which is the real world?" before assigning the paper to be written outside of class.

2. Before distributing **Handout 36** ask "When did Rosencrantz and Guildenstern die?" If no one mentions the title, do so. Read the handout. Stress the importance of examining the scenes from which the quotations are taken and of looking up the other references to death.
   Suggested Responses:
   a. *Only the Player is realistic.*
   b. *The accuracy of the other definitions depends upon the individual. Both Rosencrantz and Guildenstern do disappear (in the film they hang). Minor characters, unlike heroes, die offstage.*
   c. *Eternity apparently bothers them because it is endless and unknown, just as their lives have been.*
   d. *Only with the Tragedians is there choice, and this is in the "realistic" acted deaths. Because of the way they are presented, the possibility of their actual deaths is arguable. Do they exist in Rosencrantz and Guildenstern's world? If the actors always play someone else, then they have no identity themselves and are nothing. Therefore, according to some critics, nothing can happen to them.*

3. Distribute **Handout 37**. Mention that Sartre, in his famous existential play *No Exit*, claimed that there is no exit. The Player disputes him in his lines. Divide students into groups to discuss the ideas presented about acting and death.
   Suggested Responses:
   a. *Death is an unknown but, according to the Players, seems to be a place. There may be a religious element assumed here. Guil denies the entrance part.*
   b. *Rosencrantz and Guildenstern's inability to leave the stage suggests their inability to leave life.*

c. It is easier to believe in the appearance of something than in the real thing.

d. After all of their concern about death, their deaths, like themselves, are totally insignificant.

e. Guil thinks the Player has cheated by returning to life after dying. Perhaps his theory of an exit without an entrance was wrong.

4. Distribute **Handout 38**, which focuses on acting. The questions may be answered as class discussion, in groups, or as homework. Because of the use of *Hamlet* in the play, the reader is constantly aware that Rosencrantz and Guildenstern are actors who have not seen the script. The Tragedians know they exist only within a script.
Suggested Responses:

1. The Tragedians have contact with the outer world, understand the situation they are in, know what audiences (people? the world?) like and expect.

2. We enjoy the intensity of emotion, the suffering of others and violence. We are swayed more by fancy words than by honest ones. We prefer Terminator to Hamlet.

3. Acting is more believable than reality. We prefer the person that someone (a politician? an actor? a friend?) seems to be to what he or she really is. They refers to audiences who have made a kind of bargain with actors to believe what they see. (See movie handout.)

4. Some critics consider "We were sent for" the key sentence, suggesting that they have no choice in the matter and are manipulated like puppets. The Messenger, roughly analogous to the boy in Waiting for Godot, could be said to have given them birth.

Gerald Weales in The Reporter says, "Rosencrantz and Guildenstern are modern man in a Beckett universe, incapable of action, uncertain of identity, bullied by accident or by an order so incomprehensible that it might as well be accident."[1]

The Player comes and goes, performs, offers advice, knows where he is going. He demonstrates the realtiy of what is to come, including Rosencrantz and Guildenstern's deaths.

5. This ties into the game motif and connects with the coin-flipping episode. He is reinforcing the idea that with life and death, we have no choices.

5. Distribute **Handout 39** which associates games with the theme of alienation. This handout may be done individually, in groups, or in class discussion.
Suggested Responses:

1. Death, choice, identity, home

2. He wins, 27-3. (See Hamlet 2.2. He does ask 27 questions while with them!)

3. No. Their universe has no logic, no reason, no order.

4. Both are con tricks, although Ros reverses the question in the year-of-birth game so he will lose. In these games, unlike the coin-flipping, Rosencrantz and Guildenstern have control over the results. When Ros first plays coin-in-hand with Guil, he has no coin in either hand, but at the end, in trying to make Guil happy, he puts a coin into each hand so Guil can win.

5. Games have rules to rely upon. However, sometimes the rules do not apply; sometimes the games lead the player to expect nothing. In the game of life, their main game, no one explained the rules; there is no way to win. They are alienated both from the leader and teammates.

6. For distraction from analysis, distribute **Handout 40**, "Verbal Tennis." Based on Rosencrantz and Guildenstern's question game, this will give students a chance to think on their toes and to exercise logic. Warn them that it isn't as easy as it looks. They may follow Rosencrantz and Guildenstern's additional rule and call grunts, such as "Huh?" fouls. Make up or adjust rules if you wish. Act as the arbitrator with non-sequiturs.

---

[1]Gerald Weales, "To Be or Not to Be," *The Reporter* (November 16, 1967): 40.

Name_____
Date_____

As the Worlds Turn

Directions: Read the following analysis carefully before writing your paper.

A recent play and movie, *Noises Off*, takes place behind stage while a play is supposedly being performed on the "good" side of the set. The audience sees the back side of the set, unpainted, propped up with boards. Actors who are charming onstage are obnoxious, confused, or nasty off-stage.

In a way the play and movie illustrate the Player's comment that the actors "do onstage the things that are supposed to happen off." Off-stage would be the "real world" as opposed to the artificial world being acted out on the good side of the set.

Think about a painting of Magritte's, *The Treachery of Images*, which shows a pipe but says beneath it, "This is not a pipe." Of course it isn't. It is a painting of a pipe. Which is real?

Stoppard has set up two worlds in his play: the world of the court, inhabited by Hamlet, Claudius, Gertrude, Polonius, and Ophelia, and the boundaryless, directionless world of Rosencrantz and Guildenstern, who keep stumbling into the first world. In a play filled with questions, just as *Hamlet* is, an unspoken one here is, "Which is the real world?"

Further confusion comes when we consider another world: that of acting. Here we have the Tragedians and their performances, invariably from *Hamlet*; the scenes from *Hamlet* that pop into or merge with the play; and the final scene, which is directly from the play. Which is the real world here? In which play are Rosencrantz and Guildenstern performing?

Think about any of these worlds. Then narrow your thoughts to a specific thesis and write an insightful paper using specific examples. If you wish, your paper can answer the question, "Which is the real world?" It can discuss the Tragedian's world as a bridge between the other two. Or it can discuss any of the worlds or compare any of them.

Are Rosencrantz and Guildenstern Dead?

Directions: Refer to the scenes from which the quotes are cited when you are discussing the key statements and questions.

Ros: Am I dead?

GUIL: Yes or no?

Ros: Is there a choice? (43)

Early in the play, during the question game, Ros asks his question. Of course there is no answer given. The title says that they *are* dead. Does this mean throughout the play? If so, how do you explain it?

All through the play they discuss death, either briefly or at length. Here are some key statements that are made:

- Ros, worried about being dead in a box, says, "Eternity is a terrible thought. I mean, where's it going to end?" (71).

- Guil says, "Death followed by eternity—the worst of both worlds" (72).

- Guil says death is merely "a man failing to reappear" (84).

- Guil defines death as "the ultimate negative" (108).

- The Player tells them, "Most things end in death" and describes death as commmonplace (123).

- Just before they disappear, Guil says death is "the absence of presence" (124).

Their on-stage "deaths" agree with Guil's definitions. Does this mean his definitions are correct? Does Hamlet die when he disappears into the barrel? Are these statements all realistic ones? Are any of them? What does Guil's comment about eternity mean? Is there a choice about death? The Tragedians specialize in dying. Since they are always in costume and always performing, can they ever actually die?

You may use other comments about death found on pp. 18, 38, 39, 43, 70, 77, 79, 82, 89, 98, 110, 119, 121, 122.

Exits and Entrances

Directions: With your group, discuss the two themes presented for analysis in this handout.

"Every exit [is] an entrance somewhere else," says the Player as he explains what the Tragedians do (28).

"Death is an exit, unobstrusive and unannounced," says Guil after the Spies die "rather well" (84).

Acting and death, the two major themes of the play, are often intertwined; the Tragedians act death in many different ways and show that an acted death is far more dramatic—and believeable—than a real one.

Unlike the Spies, Rosencrantz and Guildenstern do not die rather well. They just fail to reappear. This failure is part of Guil's earlier definition of death—"Now you see him, now you don't" (84). Guil's last words before his disappearance are, "Now you see me, now you—" (126). He does not agree with the Player about an entrance following the exit. That, he says, occurs only in acted deaths, when the Player returns wearing a different hat. In real death, he says, "no one gets up" (123).

Think about these parallels: acting and death, exits and entrances. Consider these things also:

- No one believed the real death of the actor on stage, described by the Player on 84.

- The Player is always "on" and always in costume and character.

- Rosencrantz and Guildenstern never leave stage until they die (are they "on"?). Their only exit is a momentary leap in a barrel.

- The Tragedians perform Rosencrantz and Guildenstern's deaths.

- At the end of act 2, Rosencrantz and Guildenstern don't know if they want to come back—or even if they want to go. (They go.)

- The Player does get up after being supposedly killed by Guil.

- The bodies of Rosencrantz and Guildenstern are not on stage in the final scene.

- When the Player gets up after being stabbed, he says, "For a moment you thought I'd—cheated" (124).

What is Stoppard saying here about death? about acting and death? about exits and entrances? about Rosencrantz and Guildenstern's deaths?

Name_____

Date_____

On Stage

Directions: Answer the questions below:

"All the world's a stage and each must play his part," said Shakespeare, as paraphrased by a modern songwriter. Our play has three sets of actors: Rosencrantz and Guildenstern, the Tragedians, and the court. The Player calls Rosencrantz and Guildenstern "fellow artists" and later gives them the oxymoronic advice to "act natural" (66). Unfortunately they do not know what play they are in or what their roles are. The court is on stage in several ways: in *Hamlet*, all are acting (madness, love, concern, etc.); their counterparts are acting out scenes from their future lives; they are participating (acting? directing?) in Rosencrantz and Guildenstern's nameless play. In effect, two plays are occurring simultaneously: Rosencrantz and Guildenstern's and *Hamlet*.

1. Of the three groups, which seems more aware of reality? Why?

2. The Player talks at length about the audience's desire for blood, love, and rhetoric. If we are part of the audience, what is he saying about us?

3. In act 2, the Player describes the actual death on stage that was not convincing. The audience did not believe it. He says, "Audiences know what to expect, and that is what they are prepared to believe in" (84). In act 3, when Guil stabs him and he dies dramatically, he comes back to life, to great applause, and tells Guil, "You see, it *is* the kind they do believe in—it's what is expected" (123). What does this show about acting and reality?

4. Rosencrantz and Guildenstern are passive characters throughout. Even their situation is stated in the passive voice: "We were sent for." They move around and talk, but they do not act; they make feeble attempts but fail. In what sense is the Player active instead of passive?

5. Explain the Player's comment on p. 115: "Life is a gamble, at terrible odds—if it was a bet you wouldn't take it."

Name_____
Date_____

The Game of Life

Directions: Here are questions for you to consider.

Rosencrantz and Guildenstern are alienated in many ways from the world and the world around them. There is no spot for them to fit in. They express their frustration several times:

GUIL: What did you expect?

Ros: Something . . . someone . . . nothing (69).

And near the end Guil asks, "What's it all about?" (121) when he pretends to be the King—just before learning of his own fate. Ros, just before he dies, asks, "What was it all about?" (125).

After the coin comes up heads 90-odd times, Guil says, "We are now within un—, sub—, or supernatural forces" (17).

They are participating in the game of life, but they have no board, no dice, no markers, and no rules.

They play several games themselves during the play: questions, which hand has the coin, the year of one's birth. As they finish the question game Ros asks, "What's the game" and Guil asks, "What are the rules?" (44).

1. A key element of the question game is that there can be no answers. Apply that to Rosencrantz and Guildenstern's situation. What themes or motifs come up in the course of the game?

2. They play another game of sorts, questions and answers, when they practice talking to Hamlet. What happens when they play this game with Hamlet?

3. Is it possible for a coin to always come up heads? What does this occurrence suggest about their universe?

   What is the purpose of the coin-in-hand game and the year-of-birth game?

4. How do the games show alienation?

Verbal Tennis

Directions: You too can play the question game! In the movie it is played on a badminton court and becomes verbal tennis, which is shorter than verbal badminton.

Divide the class into two groups. Review the rules: the other side gets a point if you give a statement, a non-sequitur, a rhetorical statement or question, or a repeated question. Three points equals a game.

Choose a representative from each team to come to the front with their metaphorical rackets and face his/her opponent. Imagine a net. The person who serves chooses the opening topic (with team help, if desired). Service and returns must be short and quick. A neutral referee, such as your teacher, can be used to catch fouls if the players miss them. Each team can have a scorekeeper.

When a game is won, send up two more players.

Sample Exchange

A: Will we win the game tomorrow?

B: What game?

A: The one with Central.

B: Foul—statement. Aren't you playing?

A: Playing what?

B: How can you ask?

A: Foul—rhetorical question. One-one. Are you getting bored?

B: With what?

A: Did you go to the school-board meeting last night?

B: Foul—non-sequitur. Two-one. Are we getting anywhere with this?

A: Were we going anywhere with it? etc.

Lesson 10
Motifs and Movies

Objectives
- To become aware of the verbal motifs in the play and visual motifs in the movie
- To observe Stoppard's use of words
- To show the difference created by a change of medium
- To compare the play *Rosencrantz & Guildenstern Are Dead* to *Waiting for Godot*

Notes to the Teacher
The play is a virtual banquet of images, motifs, allusions, puns, and wordplay. (This lesson is limited to four motifs, some wordplay, the movie version, and one comparison exercise.) In addition may be included such points as choice, chance, indecision, coming and going, syllogisms, and the coins and, of course, parallels to *Waiting for Godot*. **Handouts 41** and **42** may be combined into one lesson. The movie, which lasts 117 minutes, is available on video. It needs to be considered a valid art form since its writer and director is the play's author. It includes far more scenes from *Hamlet* (with vast changes in the stage directions) and often moves at a confusing pace. What may trouble some students is the presenting of a non-literal, absurd play in a literal way—something like doing a movie of *Our Town* with real houses and staircases and soda fountains and cemeteries.

As a writing assignment, students may choose one or two of the motifs and show how it or they contribute to a theme.

Procedure
1. Distribute **Handout 41**. Ask students to read the page. Discuss the questions as a class.
   Suggested Responses:
   1. *A boat, like Rosencrantz and Guildenstern, is small, insignificant when at sea, isolated. One is stuck on a boat; has no choice.*
   2. *It is going full circle, not away from their problems; under the control of an invisible current and wind.*
   3. *Although he knows they are being controlled, he feels, in the first speech, a sense of freedom. In the last speech, he realizes the control is total and inexorable; they have no freedom.*

   4. *Rosencrantz and Guildenstern*
   5. *We are all like Rosencrantz and Guildenstern—lost, merely existing, out of control.*

2. Distribute **Handout 42**. Divide the class into search groups to find the uses of the motifs. Determine, as a class, the answers to the questions.
   Suggested Responses:
   Wheel: (stage directions) pp. 17, 72, 82, 88, 123; (other) 60, 108, 110, 116
   Time: pp. 16, 17, 19, 72, 76
   Home: pp. 16, 37, 38, 43, 44, 120
   1. **Wheel:** *Rosencrantz, in* Hamlet *(3.3), describes the King as a wheel to whose spokes "10,000 lesser things" are attached. All fall when the King dies. In stage directions in Rosencrantz & Guildenstern Are Dead, wheeling is done throughout the play by Ros, the Player, and especially Guil. It shows the wheeler's desperation and reinforces the idea of their going in circles. In act 2, Guil mentions wheels set in motion and realizes that he and Ros are condemned to be caught under those wheels. In act 3, wheel is mentioned several times, perhaps because they are on a boat. Guil sees himself and Ros as merely "wheels within wheels"—the big wheels being perhaps the ones that Ros wants to put a spoke in. He is not bothered by the wheels that are turning. But here the little guys die, so no one else falls when their little wheels fail to turn.*
   2. **Time:** *suspended during the coin-tossing, Time is something even the Tragedians don't have much of. Ros says, "There's only one direction, and time is its only measure." The statement is the essence of the time motif: time may seem suspended, as are the laws of probability, but even in their absurd world, their lives are limited by time, and their only direction, despite their constant confusion, is towards death.*
   3. **Home:** *They remember the fact of home but nothing about it. They want to go home but have no idea where it is. During the question game Guil asks, "What home?"*

They are from nowhere and belong no-where. They cannot go home; their thoughts must point in another direction—towards death.

3. Distribute **Handout 43**. If an audiocassette of Abbot and Costello's "Who's on First?" is available, play it for the class. Discuss the elements that make it funny. Make sure students see the humor in the handout's quoted lines. The search for codas and clichés can be done as homework, followed by discussion.
   Suggested Responses:
   1. *Coda page numbers: 39, 45, 93, 102, 114. All are variants of "Give us this day our daily bread." The phrase "all I ask" is present in all, although* ask *changes to* seek *and* presume; give *changes to* call. *They ask for consistency, immortality, a change of ground, their common due, and plausibility. They want given to them their daily mask, week, round, cue, and tune. The players give them their tune, lack of identity their mask, meaninglessness their week, fate their round, and life their cue. They get a change of ground but nothing else. They seek the unfindable through-out; their search brings them to their end.*
   2. *Cliché page numbers: 38, 74, 120. On p. 38, they maul several chlichés: "high and dry," "over my dead body," "out of my depth," "heading to a stop." Their confusion starts with home and ends with death. Ros mixes two clichés in one sentence on p. 74: "Never look a gift horse in the mouth" and "Don't shoot until you see the whites of their eyes." On p. 120, Guil finally achieves "high and dry." The twisting perhaps shows their confusion or the failure of language.*

4. Distribute **Handout 44**. The stars of the movie are Richard Dreyfuss (as the Player), Gary Oldham and Tim Roth. Guil wears a gold earring; Ros has dark hair that dangles.
   Suggested Responses:
   1. *Many more* Hamlet *scenes are used. Rosencrantz and Guildenstern are hanged. There are no barrels on the boat to jump into. Locales are added: bath-house, courtyard, painted room, etc.; puppets and oriental actors are added; Rosencrantz and Guildenstern peek into several* Hamlet *scenes, etc.*
   2. *Possible meanings:*

   a. *Wind blowing: Rosencrantz and Guildenstern are buffeted about by others, have no control*
   b. *Sheets of paper: lives are scripted*
   c. *Stairs: their meaningless, repetitive lives*
   d. *Echoes: lack of reality*
   e. *Dog howling: approach of death*

   4. *Some are dropping the ball and the feather; the apple dropping on Ros' head; Hamlet clucking to the chicken and belching; Rosencrantz and Guildenstern falling down the trap door and chasing the play-ers through halls; Ros on boat donning earplugs and mask for bed*
   5. *More prominent than in the play; he does vulgar or ridiculous things such as belch-ing, playing with a cup and ball, clucking to hens, cutting the chandelier. The movie probably has more than double the amount of time used for* Hamlet *scenes. Answers on effect will vary.*
   6. *They don't disappear. They are ready to hang. The Player has his hand on the rope.*
   7. *Reactions will depend on reactions to a literal version of the play. Masks suggest that people are not who they seem to be. Puppets suggest that the characters are mere puppets being controlled by some invisible puppeteer.*
   8. *After a while they are easy to distinguish. Ros is noticeably dense.*

5. Distribute **Handout 45**. If students have studied both plays, they can work in groups— perhaps two categories per group—and discuss as a class, or students can choose one of the categories as the basis of a com-parison paper.
   Suggested Responses:
   1. *Two main characters are inseparable and, in effect, lost. In* Rosencrantz & Guildenstern Are Dead *they are simi-lar. In* Waiting for Godot *they are comple-mentary.*
   2. *Vladimir and Estragon play Pozzo and Lucky. Pozzo performs. Everyone acts in* Rosencrantz & Guildenstern Are Dead *.*
   3. *Both plays contain several games, includ-ing word games.*
   4. *Vladimir and Estragon actually go off-stage briefly, unlike Rosencrantz and Guildenstern, but for both their lives are meaningless comings and goings—no-where.*

5. *Vladimir and Estragon know who they are. They don't know who anyone else is. Rosencrantz and Guildenstern recognize others but don't know their own names. Neither pair has any identifiable character.*
6. *Both are outside the real world.*
7. *Vladimir and Estragon cling to Godot; Rosencrantz and Guildenstern just hang on and hope.*
8. *Both do them; Rosencrantz and Guildenstern do more of them and much funnier ones.*
9. *Important in both; illogical in both*
10. *Pauses are used in both but more often in Waiting for Godot; Rosencrantz and Guildenstern have no silences.*

Rosencrantz & Guildenstern Are Dead is fairly heavy in content—much lighter than *Waiting for Godot*, though, according to many critics—but it is lighter in spirit. It moves faster; characters talk more, move more, and pause less. *Waiting for Godot* relies on silences to slow it down. Rosencrantz and Guildenstern has more characters. Both are actually or in effect all-male plays.

Name_____
Date_____

We're in the Same Boat, Brother

Directions: Read the following in preparation for discussion of the question.

Rosencrantz and Guildenstern—not to mention their friends Hamlet and the Tragedians—end up on a boat. Many lines mention or discuss boats:

a. GUIL: I'm very fond of boats myself. I like the way they're—contained. You don't have to worry about which way to go or whether to go at all. . . . One is free on a boat. For a time. Relatively. . . . Free to move, speak, extemporize, and yet. We have not been cut loose. Our truancy is defined by one fixed star, and our drift represents merely a slight change of angle to it . . . but we are brought round full circle . . . (100–101).

b. ROS: For those in peril on the sea . . . (42).

c. ROS: Do you think death could possibly be a boat?

   GUIL: No, no, no . . . Death is . . . not, . . . Not being. You can't not-be on a boat.

   ROS: I've frequently not-been on boats.

   GUIL: No, no, no—what've you've been is not on boats (108).

d. GUIL: (*hearing music*) Out of the void, finally, a sound; while on a boat (*admittedly*) outside the action (*admittedly*) the perfect and absolute silence of the wet lazy slap of water against water and the rolling creak of timber—breaks; giving rise at once to the speculation . . . that something is about to happen (112).

e. PLAYER: Aha! All in the same boat, then! (114).

f. GUIL: Where we went wrong was getting on a boat. We can move, of course, change direction, rattle about, but our movement is contained within a larger one that carries us along as inexorably as the wind and current. . . .

The boat goes far beyond just being a boat. The boat motif picks up some themes and ideas discussed earlier.

1. Why is a boat an effective motif?

2. How does the boat suggest their fate?

3. How does Guil's first speech differ from his last?

4. Whom does Ros' first statement ironically include?

5. What universal meaning does the Player's comment have?

Motifs

Directions: Search for the uses of the motifs used in the play. Stoppard intertwines a number of motifs in his work. Let us look at three to see what he accomplishes with them: Wheel, Time, and Home.

1. *Wheel*, an image borrowed from *Hamlet*, is used five times in stage directions and four times in dialogue. Find the words and determine their purpose.

2. Along with *Direction* he uses *Time* at least five times in stage directions. Find the instances, determine their purpose, and connect them with *Direction*.

3. *Home* occurs on six pages. Find the uses and their contexts and determine their purpose.

4. With what themes do these motifs connect?

More Words, Words, Words

Directions: Read the following explanation and find the codas and clichés used in the play.

> PLAYER: . . . you understand, we are tied down to a language which makes up
> in obscurity what it lacks in style.

Stoppard certainly is not tied down in his language. He uses witty wordplay throughout the play. For example:

Ros: Stark raving sane (68).

GUIL: He's a retentive King, a royal retainer (41).

GUIL: Unless we're off course.

Ros: Of course (99).

GUIL: England? *That's* a dead end (121).

The rapid-fire exchanges between Rosencrantz and Guildenstern (and sometimes the Player) may remind you of Abbott and Costello's famous comic routine "Who's on First?" Stoppard also plays with language when he has his characters dressed in Elizabethan costumes but speaking in very modern English.

Stoppard also plays with language with his *codas* and his twisted *clichés.*

1. A coda, in music, takes you to the finish. It is also the end of a literary piece that ties all the themes together. Stoppard's five codas are all rhymed couplets, occasionally separated by another line, containing some identical and similar phrases. The first occurs on p. 39. Find all five codas, examine them, compare them, and determine their purpose.

2. Both poets and comics twist clichés for different purposes. Twice (pp. 86 and 114) Stoppard uses a cliché untwisted and makes it funny by making it literal, but several other times he changes a word within the cliché. There are three twisted clichés in the play, the first (a series of them) on p. 38. Find the others, determine if they are serious or funny or both, and determine their purpose.

Name_____
Date_____

Rosencrantz & Guildenstern Are Dead: The Movie

Directions: Use these notes and questions as a guide in viewing the movie.

About twenty-five years after writing the play, Stoppard wrote and directed a movie version. He purposefully made changes in words and actions: deletions, alterations, and additions. Whereas the stage version relies mainly on words and their manipulation, the movie relies more on visual images.

As you watch the movie, think about these questions:

1. What obvious changes are in the script?

2. Notice these motifs and decide on their meanings: the wind blowing, sheets of paper (often blowing, sometimes folded), stairs, echoes, a dog howling.

3. The bare stage becomes a realistic, detailed set. They are in a real castle and on a real boat. What effect does this realism have on a play? Can an absurd play be performed in a literal way?

4. One visual joke that is added shows one of our heroes creating and eating a Dagwood-style hamburger, straight from the 20th century. What other jokes (mainly visual) do you find?

5. How predominant is Hamlet in the movie? How is he shown? Compared to the play, what portion of the movie consists of scenes from *Hamlet*? How does this affect the movie?

6. How is Rosencrantz and Guildenstern's disappearance scene changed? Does this change the play? Does it make the Player guilty of their deaths?

7. Instead of simple, on-the-spot mime shows, the movie has a dumb show with skulls, a drowning, and the sound of swords; a mime with masks, an oriental dumbshow and a puppet show; all performing scenes from *Hamlet*. At the end the mime is replaced by shots of the described actions actually happening. What is the effect of these changes? What might the use of masks and puppets suggest?

8. How difficult is it to tell Rosencrantz and Guildenstern apart in the movie?

9. What is the most effective change Stoppard made? the least?

10. Which version do you prefer? Why?

Comparison of Plays

Directions: Consider in what ways Beckett's and Stoppard's plays are similar. Since Stoppard obviously and openly used *Waiting for Godot* as a starting point for his play, many comparisons can be made. What comparisons do you see? Add to this list, if you can.

1. Characters

2. Acting

3. Games

4. Coming and going

5. Identity

6. Alienation

7. Hope

8. Music-hall routines

9. Time

10. Pauses

What differences in style do you notice?

Name_____
Date _____

Comprehension Quiz: *Waiting for Godot*

1. What is the condition of the tree in act 1?

2. Name two things Lucky carries for Pozzo.

3. How does Lucky entertain the others?

4. What specifically do all four men wear?

5. What happens to Pozzo's watch?

6. What message does Godot send?

7. What change occurs in Pozzo?

8. In act 2, to what two names does Pozzo respond besides his own?

9. In act 2, how has the tree changed?

10. Where did Estragon get the cord that they test for hanging?

Comprehension Quiz: *Rosencrantz & Guildenstern Are Dead*

1. What do the Players' audiences like to see?

2. What important thing do Rosencrantz and Guildenstern have great difficulty remembering?

3. Why did they leave their homes?

4. Name two games they play.

5. What is *death*, according to Guildenstern after seeing the players perform the deaths of the Spies?

6. In the play-within-a-play mime, what scene from *Hamlet* is acted out?

7. On the boat, what does Hamlet do when he comes to the front of the stage?

8. Where does everyone hide when the pirates come?

9. According to the stage directions, what specifically happens to both Rosencrantz and Guildenstern at the end?

10. What is the final scene?

Answer Keys to Comprehension Quizzes

Waiting for Godot

1. Barren, no leaves

2. Bag, greatcoat, picnic basket, folding stool (briefly, a whip)

3. Dances, makes a speech

4. Bowler hats

5. He loses it.

6. He'll come tomorrow.

7. He is blind.

8. Cain and Abel

9. It has four or five leaves.

10. It came from his waist—it is his belt.

Rosencrantz & Guildenstern Are Dead

1. Deaths

2. Their names

3. They were called.

4. Questions, coin toss, double the year of your age, pick the hand with the coin

5. A failure to reappear, an exit

6. The Queen's closet scene (Polonius' stabbing)

7. Spits into the audience

8. In barrels

9. They disappear.

10. The ambassadors reporting, from the end of *Hamlet*

Composition Topics: *Waiting for Godot*

1. Write a defense of Vladimir and Estragon as Everyman.

2. All of the characters wear bowlers like Charlie Chaplin's or Magritte's men. Discuss the use of hats in the play. Include when they are removed and put back on.

3. Pozzo says Vladimir and Estragon were "made in God's image!" Consider Lucky's portrait of God and other comments about God in the play. Describe man as the image of the play's God.

4. The characters are constantly falling or almost falling. Discuss the motif of falling in the play.

5. One critic says that Vladimir and Estragon have a better choice than waiting for Godot—suicide. Is this a better choice for them? Discuss.

6. The Messenger is a very minor character who enters twice haltingly and leaves both times running. Examine his appearances, his timing, and his dialogue. How is he used in the play? What is his significance?

7. Discuss Pozzo as the epitome of modern man obsessed with power and encumbered by possessions.

8. Henry David Thoreau says, "The mass of men lead lives of quiet desperation." Discuss the play as an illustration of this statement.

9. Thoreau says, "What a man thinks of himself, that it is which determines, or rather indicates, his fate." Discuss Pozzo as an illustration of this statement.

10. Become a critic! Write your interpretation of Lucky's wild speech (which is all one sentence!).

11. Discuss the implications of the Cain/Abel motif in the play.

12. The play is about waiting. What is the importance of their waiting? How does Beckett emphasize it?

13. The main characters are constantly confused about where they are and when they were there before. Discuss this confusion about time and place and its significance.

14. Estragon frequently falls asleep in the middle of discussions. What does this tendency show about him?

15. In his speech about the gravedigger, Vladimir says, "At me too someone is looking, of me too someone is saying, 'He is sleeping, he knows nothing, let him sleep on.'" Interpret this passage.

16. Examine and discuss the relationship between Pozzo and Lucky.

17. Will Godot ever come? Why or why not?

18. Discuss the tree as a symbol. If you wish, include the moon.

19. Pozzo and Lucky are going "on" when they leave. Vladimir and Estragon continue on. Where is "on"? What point is Beckett making?

20. Reread the section about the two thieves. Consider it in terms of salvation, grace, chance, and arbitrariness as shown in the play. Discuss.

21. Discuss the play in terms of its theme of the mysteriousness of existence.

22. Look at Vladimir's song about a dog at the beginning of act 2. Connect it with any themes of the play.

23. Why is the play set at twilight?

24. When the boy tells him he thinks Godot's beard is white, Vladimir responds, "Christ have mercy on us." Explain.

25. Explain what Beckett is doing with the food in the play: the chicken bones, the carrots, turnips, and radishes.

26. Listen to two of Simon and Garfunkel's songs, "Somewhere They Can't Find Me" and "Dangling Conversation." What comparisons can you make between their words and the play?

27. Discuss Vladimir and Estragon as players in the nonsense game of life.

28. What binds Vladimir and Estragon?

29. Why would this play be appealing and clear to a group of convicts? Discuss.

30. Tad Friend, in *The New Republic*, writes in defense of the middlebrow. He claims highbrow is removed from ordinary life, grand in manner, abstruse, full of boredom and depression. He says, "The question 'Who farted?' is patently lowbrow—except when Estragon poses it in *Godot*. Then it's highbrow."[1] Explain.

31. Beckett, unlike authors of novels, cannot use narrators or his own voice to affect the audience's response to the play. What techniques does he use to guide their responses (some examples: setting, comparable characters)?

32. Write a final scene for the play in which Godot comes to them. It can be funny, serious, or both.

[1]Tad Friend, "In Praise of Middlebrow," *The New Republic* (March 2, 1992): 25.

Composition Topics: *Rosencrantz & Guildenstern Are Dead*

1. Choose one character; write a character sketch that clearly distinguishes him from the other. (Use Ros or Guil only.)

2. Prove that Rosencrantz and Guildenstern are victims instead of perpetrators of their fate.

3. In 1968 in *Life*, Tom Prideaux wrote, "*Rosencrantz & Guildenstern Are Dead* proves to be an apt expression of our dilemmas and doubts. . . . Uncertainty is a sign not necessarily of a weak and wavering mind but often of a venturous mind prying out truths not simple to assess."[2] Discuss.

4. Discuss the use of significance of the codas.

5. Why is the wheel imagery appropriate for this play?

6. If the arrival of the messenger is equivalent to their birth, what is the meaning and purpose of their life, which is shown in its entirety?

7. Identity is the key to this play. What is Stoppard saying about the world through this theme?

8. On p. 94, Guil speaks of the autumnal day, using various colors to describe it. Interpret this passage.

9. Find specific lines or actions that show Rosencrantz and Guildenstern's indecisiveness. Explain what this trait shows.

10. Contrast the Player's comments about death with Guil's.

11. Choose one of the games and show how it contributes to the meaning of the play.

12. "We were sent for," says Ros several times. What is the importance of this line?

13. Characterize Hamlet as shown in this play.

14. Compare Guil's comments about death to those of the real Hamlet.

15. In *Hamlet*, Hamlet, the amateur actor, advises the professional players that the purpose of playing is, "to hold, as 'twere, the mirror up to nature. . . ." (3.3). In what sense do the Tragedians in *Rosencrantz & Guildenstern Are Dead* follow this advice?

16. Acting is a theme in both *Hamlet* and *Rosencrantz & Guildenstern Are Dead*. How do its meaning and purpose vary in the two plays?

17. Prove that Rosencrantz and Guildenstern are figuratively dead from the beginning of the play.

18. Discuss the Player's statement that every exit is an entrance somewhere else, as a theme of the play.

19. Examine the Player's comments about the plays his group performs and their other exhibition. What point is Stoppard making about today's world?

[2]Tom Prideaux, *Life* (February 9, 1968): 76.

20. In what sense are Rosencrantz and Guildenstern trapped in their situation?

21. What is the purpose and effect of having Rosencrantz and Guildenstern identified by the Player as actors?

22. Examine Rosencrantz and Guildenstern's reaction when they discover they are taking Hamlet to England to be killed. Discuss and explain their reaction.

23. In the movie, Stoppard has Rosencrantz and Guildenstern hanged instead of disappearing. Defend or attack this change.

24. The tossed coin introduces the idea of fate. Show how fate operates in the course of the play.

25. Discuss the theme of alienation in the play.

26. Discuss this statement by C.W.E. Bigsby about Shakespeare's view of man: "Man . . . is a minor character in a drama which he cannot understand, dependent for recognition on people who do not even control their fate and forces which may not even exist."[3]

27. Prove or disprove: Rosencrantz and Guildenstern fail because they are cowards.

28. Discuss: "It is only when Rosencrantz and Guildenstern step fully into the *Hamlet* play and resume their roles without resistance that they realize their [reason for existence] is those roles."[4]

29. At the end of the play, after the Player dies and comes back to life with applause, he speaks to Guil about the audience? "You see, it *is* the kind they do believe in—it's what is expected." The movie script changes *they* to *you*. What is the significance of this change?

30. Unlike Rosencrantz and Guildenstern, the players know that, in effect, they exist only in a script. When Guil asks the Player who decides who dies, the Player replies, "*Decides*? It is *written.*" Consider this as a philosophical statement and discuss the play in terms of it.

31. How does the sustained allusion to *Hamlet* enhance the play?

32. Prove that the Player has no identity.

33. Prove or disprove that the Player is the protagonist.

34. Discuss the symbolism of the blowing paper in the movie.

35. Write a review of the movie.

36. Write a first-person poem, using Ros or Guil as the speaker. Narrow it to one specific idea. Be true to the play and to his character.

---

[3]Qtd. in *Tom Stoppard,* ed. Harold Bloom (New York: Chelsea House, 1986), 75.
[4]June M. Schueter, "Moon and Birdboat, Rosencrantz and Guildenstern," in *Tom Stoppard,* Ibid., 83.

Comparative Composition Topics

1. Compare the use of messengers in the plays.

2. In what sense does *Waiting for Godot* use the wheel imagery of *Rosencrantz & Guildenstern Are Dead*?

3 How does each show life as a game with no rules?

4. How do the two pairs of men differ?

5. Compare Lucky and Albert.

6. How do the plays differ in their treatments of direction, identity, and/or alienation?

7. Both plays show that Time has no beginning, middle, or end. Prove this.

8. Both plays deal with the meaningless of life. Show how they are alike and different.

9. Read these lines from Philip Schultz's poem "My Guardian Angel Stein." Show how they apply to both plays: "Life is a comedy salted with despair. All humans are disappointed./Laugh yourself to sleep each night & with luck, pluck & credit cards/you'll beat them at their own game."[5]

10. Discuss both as Absurdist plays.

11. Explain the lack of women in both plays.

12. Write a short play or story entitled "Pozzo and the Player." Include dialogue. They can meet on one of Pozzo's journeys before he was blind or after.

13. Write a feminist version of either play.

[5]Excerpt from "My Guardian Angel Stein," Copyright © 1982 by Philip Schultz, from *Deep within the Ravine* by Philip Schultz. Used by permission of Viking Penguin, a division of Penguin Books USA Inc.

Existentialism

1. Existentialism opposes any absolutes; thus, naturalism's "I perceive; therefore, I am," is rejected as accepting the binding control of nature's laws.

2. The existentialist starts with experience first: he exists; because he exists, he thinks; he feels; he perceives.

3. Our feeling, our state, our existence is one of dread, and anxiety.

4. When the existentialist is no longer conscious of himself as being, he feels that he is nothing.

5. Because each man knows that he is free and that he is the origin of his own having, possessing, creating, and existing, he is in anguish, pain, and dread.

6. But each man is isolated, alone with his own freedom.

7. No other person or agency—except time—can take this burden, this freedom from him.

8. Man should never fool himself with any hope of future success.

9. Thus, human existence is replete with lack of fulfillment, emptiness, and frustration.

10. The existentialist believes that belief is consciousness of choosing.

11. Choice is always possible, but what is not possible is not to choose.

12. When he fulfills himself, he exists. This fulfilling can come only through the agony of choices which uphold his own self-consciousness.

13. The conviction of making choices is never one of reason, only one of intense passion: human existence is no more than passion.

14. What counts as real is the individual's inner response to a situation which he has experienced.

15. Man is absurd. He could escape his agony by suicide, alcoholism, protracted narcotic states, and other abnormal acts against human existence, but he avoids these. He prefers to live with his consciousness—certain only of uncertainty. He learns to accept and to live with the fact of death. He equates his constant negation as a death, or as reduction to nothingness.

16. Because of what I am, as an existentialist, I cannot stop time, except through death, suicide, insanity, alcoholism, or narcotics addiction.[6]

[6]Excerpted from Wesley Barnes, *The Philosophy and Literature of Existentialism* (New York: Barron's Educational Series, Inc., 1961), 91–99.

Bibliography

Stoppard

Billington, Michael. *Stoppard the Playwright.* New York: Heineman, 1988.

Bloom, Harold, ed. and intro. *Tom Stoppard.* (Modern Critical Views Series). New York: Chelsea House, 1986.

Delany, Paul. *Tom Stoppard: The Moral Vision of the Major Plays.* New York: St. Martin's Press, 1990.

Hartz, John III. *Tom Stoppard: A Casebook.* (Casebook on Modern Dramatists—Garland Reference Library of the Humanities). Garland Publishing Co., 1988.

Jenkins, Anthony. *Critical Essays of Tom Stoppard.* (Critical Essays on British Literature Series). Boston: G.K. Hall, 1990.

Kelly, Katherine E. *Tom Stoppard and the Craft of Comedy: Medium and Genre at Play.* Ann Arbor: University of Michigan Press, 1990.

Rusinko, Susan. *Tom Stoppard.* (Twayne's English Authors Series: 419). Boston: G.K. Hall, 1986.

Magritte

Breton, Andre. *Magritte.* Institute for the Arts, 1964.

Gablik, Suzi. *Magritte.* (World of Art Series). Thames Hudson, 1984.

Hammacher, A.M. *Magritte.* (Masters of Art Series). New York: Abrams, 1986.

Hughes, Robert. "The Poker-Faced Enchanter," *Time* (September 21, 1992): 62–63.

Magritte 1992. New York: te Neues Publishing Co., 1991. (an illustrated appointment calendar book)

Plagers, P. "The Absolut Magritte," *Newsweek* (July 6, 1992): 50–51.

Sylvester, David. *Magritte: The Silence of the World.* New York: Harry Abrams, Inc. Publishing, 1992.

Smithsonian Magazine (September 1992): 49–57.

Torczyner, Harry. *Magritte: The True Art of Painting.* New York: Abrams, 1985.

Beckett

Astro, Alan. *Understanding Samuel Beckett.* (Understanding Modern European and Latin American Literature Series).

Ben-Zvi, Linda. *Samuel Beckett.* (Twayne English Authors Series. #423). Boston: G.K. Hall, 1986.

Bloom, Harold, ed. *Samuel Beckett's Waiting for Godot.* (Modern Critical Interpretation Series). New York: Chelsea House, 1987.

Busi, Frederick. *The Transformations of Godot*. Louisville: The University Press of Kentucky, 1980.

Esslin, Martin, ed. *Samuel Beckett: A Collection of Critical Essays*. Englewood Cliffs, N.J.: Prentice-Hall, Inc., 1965.

Esslin, Martin. *The Theatre of the Absurd*. New York: Anchor Books, 1961.

Fletcher, John and Beryl S. *A Student's Guide to the Plays of Samuel Beckett*. New York: Faber and Faber, 1990.

Fletcher, John. *Samuel Beckett's Art*. New York: Barnes & Noble, 1967.

Graver, Laurence. *Samuel Beckett: Waiting for Godot*. (Landmarks of World Literature Series). Cambridge: Cambridge University Press, 1989.

Webb, Eugene. *The Plays of Samuel Beckett*. Seattle: University of Washington Press, 1974.

Philosophy

Barnes, Wesley, *The Philosophy and Literature of Existentialism*. New York: Barron's Educational Series, Inc., 1968.

Acknowledgments

For permission to reprint all works in this volume, grateful acknowledgment is made to the following holders of copyright, publishers, or representatives.

Lesson 1, Handout 2
Painting in black and white by Marc Chagall, *Peasant Life*, 1925, oil on canvass, 39–3/8" x 31–1/2," Albright-Knox Art Gallery, Buffalo, New York, Room of Contemporary Art Fund, 1941.

Lesson 1, Handout 4
Two paintings in black and white by René Magritte, *Golconde* (1953) and *L'empire des lumières* (1954) from The Menil Collection, Houston, Texas. Reprinted with permission.

Lesson 1, Handout 5
Excerpts from *The Annotated Alice* by Lewis Carroll. Published by Clarkson N. Potter, Inc., New York, New York, 1960.

Lesson 1, Handout 8
"Don't Let That Horse" by Laurence Ferlinghetti from *A Coney Island of the Mind* by Laurence Ferlinghetti. Copyright © 1958 by Laurence Ferlinghetti. Reprinted by permission of New Directions Publishing Corp.

Lesson 2, Handout 10
"Polonius" by Miroslav Holub from *Miroslav Holub: Selected Poems*, translated by Ian Milner and George Theiner (Penguin Books, 1967). Copyright © Miroslav Holub, 1967, translation © Penguin Books Ltd., 1967.

Lesson 2, Handout 11
"The End of the World" by Archibald MacLeish from *The Collected Poems of Archibald MacLeish*, copyright 1952 by Archibald MacLeish. Reprinted by permission of Houghton Mifflin Company, New York, New York.

Excerpts from *Waiting for Godot* by Samuel Beckett. Copyright 1954, 1982 by Samuel Beckett. Reprinted with permission of Grove Press.

Excerpts from *Rosencrantz & Guildenstern Are Dead* by Tom Stoppard. Copyright 1967 by Tom Stoppard. Reprinted with permission of Grove Press, Inc.

Supplementary Materials
Excerpts from *The Philosophy and Literature of Existentialism* by Wesley Barnes. Published 1961 by Barron's Educational Series, Inc., Hauppauge, New York.

Excerpt from "My Guardian Angel" in *Deep within the Ravine* by Philip Schultz. Published 1984 by Penguin USA, New York, New York.

Novel/Drama Series

Novel

Across Five Aprils, Hunt

Adam of the Road, Gray/Catherine, Called Birdy, Cushman

The Adventures of Huckleberry Finn, Twain

The Adventures of Tom Sawyer, Twain

Alice's Adventures in Wonderland/ Through the Looking-Glass, Carroll

All Creatures Great and Small, Herriot

All Quiet on the Western Front, Remarque

All the King's Men, Warren

Animal Farm, Orwell/ The Book of the Dun Cow, Wangerin, Jr.

Anna Karenina, Tolstoy

Anne Frank: The Diary of a Young Girl, Frank

Anne of Green Gables, Montgomery

April Morning, Fast

The Assistant/The Fixer, Malamud

The Autobiography of Miss Jane Pittman, Gaines

The Awakening, Chopin/ Madame Bovary, Flaubert

Babbitt, Lewis

The Bean Trees/Pigs in Heaven, Kingsolver

Beowulf/Grendel, Gardner

Black Boy, Wright

Billy Budd/Moby Dick, Melville

Bless Me, Ultima, Anaya

Brave New World, Huxley

The Bridge of San Luis Rey, Wilder

The Brothers Karamazov, Dostoevsky

The Call of the Wild/White Fang, London

The Canterbury Tales, Chaucer

The Catcher in the Rye, Salinger

The Cay/Timothy of the Cay, Taylor

Charlotte's Web, White/ The Secret Garden, Burnett

The Chosen, Potok

The Christmas Box, Evans/ A Christmas Carol, Dickens

Chronicles of Narnia, Lewis

Cold Sassy Tree, Burns

The Count of Monte Cristo, Dumas

Crime and Punishment, Dostoevsky

Cry, the Beloved Country, Paton

Dandelion Wine, Bradbury

Darkness at Noon, Koestler

David Copperfield, Dickens

A Day No Pigs Would Die, Peck

Death Comes for the Archbishop, Cather

December Stillness, Hahn/ Izzy, Willy-Nilly, Voigt

The Divine Comedy, Dante

The Dollmaker, Arnow

Don Quixote, Cervantes

Dr. Zhivago, Pasternak

Dubliners, Joyce

East of Eden, Steinbeck

Emma, Austen

Fahrenheit 451, Bradbury

A Farewell to Arms, Hemingway

Farewell to Manzanar, Houston & Houston/Black Like Me, Griffin

Frankenstein, Shelley

From the Mixed-up Files of Mrs. Basil E. Frankweiler, Konigsburg/The Westing Game, Raskin

A Gathering of Flowers, Thomas, ed.

The Giver, Lowry

The Good Earth, Buck

The Grapes of Wrath, Steinbeck

Great Expectations, Dickens

The Great Gatsby, Fitzgerald

Gulliver's Travels, Swift

Hard Times, Dickens

Hatchet, Paulsen/Robinson Crusoe, Defoe

The Heart Is a Lonely Hunter, McCullers

Heart of Darkness, Conrad

Hiroshima, Hersey/On the Beach, Shute

The Hobbit, Tolkien

Homecoming/Dicey's Song, Voigt

The Hound of the Baskervilles, Doyle

The Human Comedy/ My Name Is Aram, Saroyan

Incident at Hawk's Hill, Eckert/ Where the Red Fern Grows, Rawls

Jane Eyre, Brontë

Johnny Tremain, Forbes

Journey of the Sparrows, Buss/Cubias/ The Honorable Prison, de Jenkins

The Joy Luck Club, Tan

Jubal Sackett/The Walking Drum, L'Amour

Julie of the Wolves, George/Island of the Blue Dolphins, O'Dell

The Jungle, Sinclair

The Killer Angels, Shaara

Le Morte D'Arthur, Malory

The Learning Tree, Parks

Les Miserables, Hugo

The Light in the Forest/ A Country of Strangers, Richter

Little House in the Big Woods/ Little House on the Prairie, Wilder

Lord of the Flies, Golding

The Lord of the Rings, Tolkien

The Martian Chronicles, Bradbury

Missing May, Rylant/The Summer of the Swans, Byars

Mrs. Mike, Freedman/I Heard the Owl Call My Name, Craven

Murder on the Orient Express/ And Then There Were None, Christie

My Antonia, Cather

The Natural, Malamud/Shoeless Joe, Kinsella

Nectar in a Sieve, Markandaya/ The Woman Warrior, Kingston

Night, Wiesel

A Night to Remember, Lord/Streams to the River, River to the Sea, O'Dell

1984, Orwell

Number the Stars, Lowry/Friedrich, Richter

Obasan, Kogawa

The Odyssey, Homer

The Old Man and the Sea, Hemingway/Ethan Frome, Wharton

The Once and Future King, White

O Pioneers!, Cather/The Country of the Pointed Firs, Jewett

Ordinary People, Guest/ The Tin Can Tree, Tyler

The Outsiders, Hinton/ Durango Street, Bonham

The Pearl/Of Mice and Men, Steinbeck

The Picture of Dorian Gray, Wilde/ Dr. Jekyll and Mr. Hyde, Stevenson

The Pigman/The Pigman's Legacy, Zindel

A Portrait of the Artist as a Young Man, Joyce

The Power and the Glory, Greene

A Prayer for Owen Meany, Irving

Pride and Prejudice, Austen

The Prince, Machiavelli/*Utopia,* More

The Prince and the Pauper, Twain

Profiles in Courage, Kennedy

Rebecca, du Maurier

The Red Badge of Courage, Crane

The Return of the Native, Hardy

A River Runs Through It, Maclean

*Roll of Thunder, Hear My Cry/
Let the Circle Be Unbroken,* Taylor

Saint Maybe, Tyler

Sarum, Rutherfurd

The Scarlet Letter, Hawthorne

A Separate Peace, Knowles

*Shabanu: Daughter of the Wind/
Haveli,* Staples

Shane, Schaefer/*The Ox-Bow
Incident,* Van Tilburg Clark

Siddhartha, Hesse

*The Sign of the Chrysanthemum/
The Master Puppeteer,* Paterson

*The Signet Classic Book of Southern
Short Stories,* Abbott and
Koppelman, eds.

The Slave Dancer, Fox/
I, Juan de Pareja, De Treviño

Song of Solomon, Morrison

The Sound and the Fury, Faulkner

Spoon River Anthology, Masters

*A Stranger is Watching/I'll be Seeing
You,* Higgins Clark

The Stranger/The Plague, Camus

Summer of My German Soldier, Greene/
Waiting for the Rain, Gordon

A Tale of Two Cities, Dickens

Talking God/A Thief of Time, Hillerman

Tess of the D'Urbervilles, Hardy

Their Eyes Were Watching God,
Hurston

Things Fall Apart/No Longer at Ease,
Achebe

To Kill a Mockingbird, Lee

To the Lighthouse, Woolf

Travels with Charley, Steinbeck

Treasure Island, Stevenson

A Tree Grows in Brooklyn, Smith

Tuck Everlasting, Babbitt/
Bridge to Terabithia, Paterson

The Turn of the Screw/Daisy Miller,
James

Uncle Tom's Cabin, Stowe

Walden, Thoreau/*A Different
Drummer,* Kelley

Walk Two Moons, Creech

Walkabout, Marshall

Watership Down, Adams

When the Legends Die, Borland

Where the Lilies Bloom, Cleaver/
No Promises in the Wind, Hunt

Winesburg, Ohio, Anderson

The Witch of Blackbird Pond, Speare/
My Brother Sam Is Dead, Collier
and Collier

A Wrinkle in Time, L'Engle/*The Lion,
the Witch and the Wardrobe,* Lewis

Wuthering Heights, Brontë

The Yearling, Rawlings/
The Red Pony, Steinbeck

Year of Impossible Goodbyes, Choi/*So
Far from the Bamboo Grove,* Watkins

Zlata's Diary, Filipović/
The Lottery Rose, Hunt

Drama

Antigone, Sophocles

Arms and the Man/Saint Joan, Shaw

The Crucible, Miller

Cyrano de Bergerac, Rostand

Death of a Salesman, Miller

A Doll's House/Hedda Gabler, Ibsen

The Glass Menagerie, Williams

The Importance of Being Earnest,
Wilde

Inherit the Wind, Lawrence and Lee

Long Day's Journey into Night, O'Neill

A Man for All Seasons, Bolt

Medea, Euripides/*The Lion in Winter,*
Goldman

The Miracle Worker, Gibson

Murder in the Cathedral, Eliot/*Galileo,*
Brecht

The Night Thoreau Spent in Jail,
Lawrence and Lee

Oedipus the King, Sophocles

Our Town, Wilder

*The Playboy of the Western World/
Riders to the Sea,* Synge

Pygmalion, Shaw

A Raisin in the Sun, Hansberry

1776, Stone and Edwards

She Stoops to Conquer, Goldsmith/
The Matchmaker, Wilder

A Streetcar Named Desire, Williams

Tartuffe, Molière

*Three Comedies of American Family
Life: I Remember Mama,* van
Druten/*Life with Father,* Lindsay
and Crouse/*You Can't Take It with
You,* Hart and Kaufman

Waiting for Godot, Beckett/
*Rosencrantz & Guildenstern Are
Dead,* Stoppard

Shakespeare

As You Like It

Hamlet

Henry IV, Part I

Henry V

Julius Caesar

King Lear

Macbeth

The Merchant of Venice

A Midsummer Night's Dream

Much Ado about Nothing

Othello

Richard III

Romeo and Juliet

The Taming of the Shrew

The Tempest

Twelfth Night

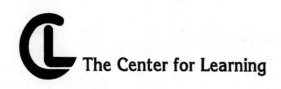
The Center for Learning

To Order Contact: **The Center for Learning—Shipping/Business Office**
P.O. Box 910 • Villa Maria, PA 16155
800-767-9090 • 412-964-8083 • Fax 888-767-8080

The Publisher

All instructional materials identified by the TAP® (Teachers/Authors/Publishers) trademark are developed by a national network of teachers whose collective educational experience distinguishes the publishing objective of The Center for Learning, a non-profit educational corporation founded in 1970.

Concentrating on values-related disciplines, The Center publishes humanities and religion curriculum units for use in public and private schools and other educational settings. Over 500 language arts, social studies, novel/drama, life issues, and faith publications are available.

While acutely aware of the challenges and uncertain solutions to growing educational problems, The Center is committed to quality curriculum development and to the expansion of learning opportunities for all students. Publications are regularly evaluated and updated to meet the changing and diverse needs of teachers and students. Teachers may offer suggestions for development of new publications or revisions of existing titles by contacting

The Center for Learning

Administrative/Editorial Office
21590 Center Ridge Road
Rocky River, Ohio, 44116
(440) 331-1404 • FAX (440) 331-5414
E-mail: cfl@stratos.net
Web: http://www.centerforlearning.org

For a free catalog, containing order and price information, and a descriptive listing of titles, contact

The Center for Learning

Shipping/Business Office
P.O. Box 910
Villa Maria, PA 16155
(412) 964-8083 • (800) 767-9090
FAX (888) 767-8080

Educator's Evaluation

The Center for Learning concept calls for frequent updates and revisions. Teachers writing for teachers will give us the best in instructional material.

Book Title _____

Excellent	Good	Fair	Poor	Criteria
				Overall effectiveness of the book
				Usability of the book
				Pacing of the material
				Quality of format and layout
				Availability of the selected text materials
				Student evaluation of the material
				Student motivation and interest
				Ability level of students
				Student achievement in the Unit

Used in Grade(s) _____

Used for
❏ Basic/Core for instruction
❏ Selected use
❏ Supplemental use

Teacher's experience
❏ 0-5 years
❏ 6-10 years
❏ 11-15 years
❏ 16 or more years

School Location
❏ large city
❏ suburb
❏ small town
❏ country

School Enrollment
❏ 1-499 students
❏ 500-999 students
❏ 1000 or more students

What is the greatest strength of this book?

What would you change in this book?

Additional Comments:

Name _____

Position _____

School _____

Address _____

Please return to:

CL The Center for Learning

**21590 Center Ridge Rd.
Rocky River, Ohio 44116**